25-101

684.104
SAV   SAVAGE, Jessie D

         Professional furniture refinishing for the
         amateur. N.Y., Harper & Row [c1975]
         202p. illus.

         1. Furniture finishing I. tc.

TT199.4.S27   S14107-30 CS

Professional Furniture Refinishing
for the Amateur

Professional Furniture Refinishing for the Amateur

JESSIE D. SAVAGE

HARPER & ROW, PUBLISHERS

NEW YORK   EVANSTON   SAN FRANCISCO

LONDON

1817

To the five
who became three
and soon to be two

FIRST EDITION

Designed by C. Linda Dingler

Library of Congress Cataloging in Publication Data

Savage, Jessie D
   Professional furniture refinishing for the amateur.
   Includes index.
   1. Furniture finishing. I. Title.
TT199.4.S27   684.1'0443   74-20414
ISBN 0-06-013774-6

75 76 77 78 79 10 9 8 7 6 5 4 3 2 1

Contents

From the Author   vii

I.   The Basics of Refinishing

II.   The Processes of Refinishing

III.   Furniture—Knowing It and Getting It

From the Author

Friends and customers ask one question beyond any others: "How did *you* get into refinishing?" Of course, the *you* means "a woman." I must admit that in these days of women's liberation, this question is asked less frequently than it was. However, you may be wondering, too, so here is the answer.

Years ago when I began to appreciate fine old furniture I also developed a desire to be able to refinish and restore it. Being a woman didn't make it easy. People didn't take my seriousness seriously. Hard facts were harder to come by.

Good, informative publications were scarce to nonexistent. Refinishers were secretive about their craft. My husband swore off the whole business because of the hard work and tremendous mess of stripping. Refinishing might have remained a sometime hobby except for one very fine fellow.

A refinisher by the name of Hamilton was the exception who proved the rule. He was good and kind enough to allow me to watch his processes and ask a thousand questions. More importantly, he introduced me to no-wash removers. I was so impressed that I bought a piece to try it on. My husband's reaction to my newly acquired pie safe was something in the form of a groan.

That pie safe was the first piece that was "all mine." There have been many others since. My first job was adequate, and each succeeding one was better because I continued to try new things and read and ask questions. Even my mistakes turned out all right. If they didn't, I would redo them until they did.

Now they turn out right the first time except, perhaps, when I'm trying some new and far-out procedure. I have tackled everything from a candlestick to a grand piano and each piece gives me a strong feeling of satisfaction.

Suddenly I discovered that I was doing more consulting work than actual refinishing. Remembering my own difficulties in getting reliable and complete refinishing information, the idea for this book grew. I turned my husband from a sometime repairman into a literary adviser and began. You see the result.

It is my hope that this effort will bring to others the pleasures of refinishing that I have enjoyed.

JESSIE D. SAVAGE

Franklin, Virginia

I

The Basics of Refinishing

1

The Basic Basics of Refinishing

The fact that you are reading this book shows that you are interested in refinishing. You have the right book—clear and complete refinishing instructions that have previously been considered complex, obscure, or even secret.

This is *not* a book about antiques or about the growing hobby of collecting them. We will not argue over the distinctions between, or the worthiness of, antiques, old furniture, or plain used furniture. Antique or "junquetique," you will find here how to repair, refinish, and restore it.

In this chapter we will answer some of the fundamental questions asked by beginning refinishers. We will warn you about some types of poor advice that you may receive. Then we will show how this book is organized for the beginner and the experienced refinisher alike and advise you on how to use it most effectively. First, some answers for the novice.

"Can I actually refinish a piece of furniture?" We can only help you answer this question for yourself. If you have the two basic qualities needed for refinishing, the answer is obviously "Yes."

The first quality needed is the ability to understand and follow simple directions. It is very important that the beginning refinisher stick to the instructions every step of the way. Even the experienced refinisher should follow directions when using a new process. There is plenty of time to experiment after one has a thorough understanding of a process and the normal result it produces. One almost sure way to ruin a job is to try something different before knowing how it should be done correctly. It is a matter of knowing all the rules in order to know when to break them. So the first prerequisite is the ability to follow instructions.

The other basic ability needed to refinish furniture is the capacity for some physical exertion. Most of the processes require far more finesse than brute force, but there is an occasional need for strength. When working with larger pieces there is a need to twist, turn, and upset them to expose all working surfaces. There are a few processes used from time to time that require a good deal of muscle power. Even these, however, may be carried out in smaller phases rather than completed all at once.

With these two fundamental qualities, anyone can refinish furniture—women as well as men. In fact, it is our belief that women generally make the best refinishers since they frequently have more patience than do men.

"Must I have a shop in which to refinish?" Apparently there are a large number of people who would like to do some refinishing but they have not because they have no workshop. This is no reason to hesitate. A workshop is convenient but it is far from necessary. A spare room, a garage, or a basement can be ideal. *Any* location can be used so long as it can be well ventilated (this is extremely important during the stripping process, as will be discussed later). A storage room can be used quite successfully.

A carport will serve well most of the year if provision can be made to protect the work-piece from driving rain. We know one dealer–refinisher in the mid-South who does all such work outside under the trees in the spring, summer, and fall.

Of course, any room in the house can be used. A grand piano, for example, is not something that one would want to cart around. It is usually refinished right where it stands, protecting the floor and nearby walls and furniture with large sheets of plastic drop cloths, as painters call them.

The lack of an ideal location for refinishing should be no deterrent to plunging into the job. Just pick any spot that is or can be well ventilated and that can remain messed up for several days at a time.

"Would I have to have a full day or several consecutive full days to refinish a piece?" As far as refinishing *per se* is concerned, time is of no importance. Large or consecutive blocks of time are *not* necessary. While a small chest can be refinished in about three days, it may be refinished quite as well in three weeks or three months or three years! A few processes, such as applying a coat of

varnish, should be completed in "one sitting," but most of them can be performed in increments of time as small as one wishes.

Time intervals between processes may be as great or as small as is convenient to the refinisher. From a practical standpoint, the time taken on a given piece will depend on two factors: how long you can tolerate waiting before putting the piece into use, and how long you can leave the work area messed up.

"How quickly can I refinish a piece?"   Minimum times are difficult to state because so much depends on exactly what must be done to the piece. However, the minimum time for stripping, staining, and finishing *anything* will be about two days. Not that an occasional table, for example, will require two and a half days of work, but several drying periods must be allowed before subsequent processes can be started.

For your guidance and with the understanding that they are only approximations for typical pieces, the following minimum times are given:

3 days—anything from a candlestick up to and including a small chest, occasional table, night stand, plain chair, small toy chest, mirror frame

5 days—medium plain or small fancy chest, large bookcase, bed, washstand, small trunk, tilt-top table

7 days—dining table, secretary, large sideboard, chifferobe, small piano, pie safe, game table, highboy

10 days—grand piano, pump organ, rolltop desk

The beginning refinisher should view the foregoing times with a very critical eye. Appearances can be deceiving, as, for example, was the case with a night stand we well remember because an anticipated three-day job was in the shop for two weeks due to concealed splits and peeling veneer, among other problems.

"Is refinishing furniture an expensive process?"   The expense depends on who is doing the refinishing. Commercial refinishers are never inexpensive, and they can be *very* expensive. Obviously, the quality of the refinishing varies from one establishment to another, and quality does not necessarily depend on the cost.

The amateur refinisher can do his own work at a cost of one-tenth to one-fourth the commercial cost. The difference is what the professional charges for his knowledge, time, and effort. Your knowledge is in this book. If you don't pay yourself for your time and effort, you will save three-fourths to nine-tenths of the cost. And you know what quality you get.

"What tools will I need?" Let us slay one dragon right here: No power tools are needed in refinishing furniture. In fact, we strongly urge that none be used even if they are available (more about that later). A few items of equipment will be needed for some of the repairing processes, but these are simple hand tools, commonly available and inexpensive. The few necessary tools are identified in the processing chapters, where their uses are described.

Of course, the well-heeled can spend a fair amount of money on tools. A full range of sizes and types of cabinetmakers' clamps, for instance, is rather expensive. They would be useful, though one can do nicely without them. So you can spend as much or as little as you want to.

"What supplies will I need to refinish a piece?" This is the most important question of all. Most of this book will be devoted to answering this question and telling how to use those supplies. Information on the selection of supplies is very difficult for the beginner to acquire.

The problem is not where to find supplies but what to buy. Even in a small store the refinisher is faced with a dazzling array of products—literally dozens of kinds of strippers, stains, fillers, sealers, varnishes, and so on.

Reading the labels will disclose that most products are the best for every task, including getting rockets to the moon. Asking the clerk will disclose that he knows less than you, cheerfully swears that the most expensive is best for whatever you want to do, and has never attempted to use any of them. Asking the professional refinisher will disclose that he won't tell you his trade secrets, and he uses supplies from containers that are unmarked or painted over. Even worse, he may give you bum advice, hoping that you'll get disgusted and bring the piece to him. Reading typical "how-to-do-it" literature will get you the run-around.

Perhaps this sounds harsh, but we have seen it happen time and again. Straight information is hard to find. We believe that the time has come to put an end to secrets, misleading information, and descriptions that beat all around the bush without saying much. We believe that *you* deserve better.

Accordingly, we have broken with tradition and named brand names. In the processing chapters, when supplies are listed and discussed, you will find the names of the specific brands we use. This has been done in every instance in which we have found that the brand makes a difference. In some cases the brand does not matter, and we say so. In some cases the brand does matter, and we say that, too.

We don't say that the specified brands are necessarily the best, since we do not claim to have tried all of those available. They *are* the ones we have found to produce quality results. They *are* the ones we use after having tried many others. Some of the products we use are the most expensive on the shelf and some are the least expensive, but most fall somewhere in the middle. You are free, of course, to use any products you wish, but you will know which ones work for us.

"What kind of piece should I use for my very first project?"

We recommend that the first refinishing project be a rather small piece. Something like a night stand, an occasional table, or a candlestick table will prove ideal. A large piece could discourage the beginner.

The selected piece should be rather plain with little carving or other ornamentation. Further, it should be in fair condition. There will be plenty of time to master all the processes without tackling them all right at the outset.

"Are there things which I should not *do?"* This is a very important question. Frankly, there is a great deal of bad advice given to beginning refinishers. Some of it is so bad that it will cause irreparable damage to fine furniture.

We live in an age of instant experts. They may be found in stores, on the printed page, and even in many refinishing shops. The beginner must remember that it is really quite easy to turn a fine piece into junk.

Listed below are the major "do nots" of refinishing. Any author, clerk, or friend who advises doing any of them should be treated with suspicion. His other advice may be good, but how can you be sure?

1. "Use sandpaper." "Use a power sander."

    If a piece has any value due to age, it should *never* be touched with sandpaper. This is because of the *patina,* which is discussed later. Sandpaper is a construction tool, suitable for use on new furniture and old junk. The use of a power sander is an extra-quick way to produce junk.

2. "Use a plane." "Use a metal scraper." "Use a scraper fashioned from broken glass."

Planes and scrapers are construction tools. On good pieces they cause the same damage as sandpaper, plus producing surfaces with gouges and hills and valleys.

3. "Replace this part with some of that."

Arbitrary and unnecessary replacement of parts destroys value. A potentially fine pie safe becomes a worthless storage cabinet when its pierced tin is replaced with glass.

4. "Remove this part with a saw or chisel."

Sawing off legs, arms, top, or whatever is an even quicker way to produce junk than by using a power sander. You may have a novelty, but you do not have a piece of good furniture.

5. "Stripping off the old finish is easy."

Not so! Stripping is work—hard work if you do it wrong. Sometimes it is hard work even when you do it right. We have discovered no easy way in over twenty years of searching. (See Chapter 5 for a discussion of commercial stripping vat processes.)

The buyer of refinished furniture should be especially alert for signs that any of these things have been done to a piece. We have found antique dealers who even boasted that a piece had been planed and sanded. Buy such pieces if you wish, but we strongly advise that you pay accordingly.

"Why should I go to all this trouble and do my own refinishing?"

People of all sizes, shapes, ages, and circumstances refinish furniture. There are almost as many reasons for refinishing as there are people who do it. For some, furniture refinishing is a satisfying and productive hobby. Many of us today earn our livelihoods in jobs that produce only intangible results. We have an unsatisfied inner need to produce something tangible—something we can touch and say (at least to ourselves) *I did that.* Few things can give this satisfaction the way a beautifully refinished chair or chest can, for example.

Another reason for refinishing is that it saves money. Old pieces can be bought "in the rough" far less expensively than is possible if they have been refinished. Refinishing itself is an expensive process when someone else does it, whether before or after you acquire a piece. The supplies used are inexpensive but the labor is not. It is like cutting your lawn: The cost of the supplies (gas and oil) is negligible, yet the boy next door charges you several dollars to do the job. Do it yourself and it costs only a few cents. Thus, if you do your own refinishing, you can have fine old pieces even though your means are limited.

Some people refinish furniture for the simple reason that they want it done correctly and well. They do the work themselves so that they can have full control of the quality of both the work and the materials used. There are a lot of slipshod "professional" refinishers around today. After taking a close, critical look at a few pieces that your friends have *had* done, what you see may be enough to send you to your own workshop.

Consider the matter of furniture quality. Aside from antiques themselves, used furniture has very little market value. Yet this same old furniture that people (and stores that have "taken it in on trade") can hardly give away is often better made than all but the most expensive new furniture. Solid, well-constructed, and quality-finished new furniture is actually hard to find. Even the most expensive lines in many stores are poorly finished. Oh, the finish *looks* all right in the showroom, but it is thin, fragile, and quickly ruined by water and alcohol. There should be a moral here somewhere, and there is.

Newlyweds (or oldlyweds) who can do their own refinishing are in the enviable position of being able to furnish an entire house with quality furniture with a very small financial investment. It cannot be done overnight, for refinishing a houseful of furniture is a time-consuming undertaking. The result, however, will be quality furniture that will last a lifetime and then some.

The final reason we shall mention for refinishing is to *make* money. Good professional refinishers are not as plentiful as one might assume. Many a do-it-yourselfer has fallen, more or less, into a profitable sideline. (We will tell you later how you can do so.) Friends who see your work in your home may ask you to refinish something for them. Their friends, in turn, ask you to do a piece. Word spreads quickly in this age of antique collecting, for nearly everyone has at least one piece that should be redone. Thus, the amateur who wishes to turn part-time professional soon finds that he has as little or as much business as he has time for. Even the slipshod refinishing shop charges plenty for its work, so the good part-time refinisher can make a nice extra income. While such income can be used for any purpose, of course, many home refinishers use it to increase their own collections.

Yes, there are as many reasons for refinishing furniture as there are people who are doing it. The reason is actually of little importance. The fact is that someone in most families has refinished a piece of furniture at one time or another. Many more pieces are in need of refinishing. If it is going to be done, it should be done well, since only a little more time is required for a quality job than is required for one fit only for the basement or garage.

"I don't plan to do any refinishing. Why should I be concerned with all this?"   Oh, how the dealers and refinishers like to see you coming! They can tell you almost anything and you will believe it. They can (and many will) charge you for your lack of knowledge and their own imaginations.

If you are buying old furniture in the rough, you need a general understanding of refinishing even though you will have someone else do it. You must be able to assess accurately the refinishing potential that may or may not exist in the pieces under consideration in order to avoid later problems. You should not have to take the word of the little-old-lady dealer who smiles sweetly and says that just a damp cloth will restore a piece to its original beauty.

If you are buying refinished pieces, you need a knowledge of refinishing. You should be able to judge for yourself the quality of the work that has been done. Then you won't pay varnish prices for lacquer work.

If you are having Aunt Hattie's gift refinished commercially, you can protect yourself from the unscrupulous fellows who infest every field of human endeavor. The nonrefinisher need no longer pay ridiculous prices for quick clean-up jobs.

If you never have or plan to have anything to do with old furniture, you obviously have picked up the wrong book. If you got the right one, here's how to use it.

Using This Book

This book contains far more information than any one person would use in several years of refinishing. There are nine basic processes that we shall discuss, but no one refinishing job uses all of them. Each process includes several phases and a number of potential problems. Just as there are many ways to go from the East Coast to the West Coast, there are many ways to turn a rough piece of furniture into a refinished piece.

There are not only parallel routes from rough to refinished, but each has a number of spurs and sidings all along the way. It is for this reason that typical refinishing literature is so confusing to the beginner. This book contains the information, but it is organized in such a manner that the reader can find what he needs for a particular job and ignore the rest. This book, like Gaul, is divided into three parts.

Part I, consisting of Chapters 1 through 4, contains the general information needed by everyone who is going to do any refinishing at all. It provides the basic background that will enable the reader to decide on the type of end product (destination) he wants and, then, to determine the best means (route) for achieving it. This section culminates in the "Refinisher's Pathfinder," which has been specifically designed as a road map through the section that follows.

In Part II, Chapters 5 through 12, the eight refinishing processes are discussed in clarity and detail. Each process is located on the "Pathfinder" and its purpose and result are stated. After a consideration of the tools and supplies needed, full and explicit instructions for the process are given. The final chapter of Part II covers the application of these processes to the special problems of restoring old finishes.

In Part III, Chapters 14 through 17 contain information that will enable the refinisher to make judgments about furniture, to evaluate the authenticity, and to have a good basis for determining the value of a piece. Chapter 18 contains information on starting a refinishing business.

2

Refinishing, Restoring, and Finishing

This is a book on refinishing both in title and in content. There are, however, two procedures so closely allied with refinishing that they cannot be ignored. With only minor changes in some of his processes, the refinisher may also be a restorer or a finisher. The purpose of this chapter is to establish clearly the interrelationships that exist among the processes involved in refinishing, restoring, and finishing.

To avoid confusion, one must first understand the way in which the word *finish* is used. This noun has two distinct meanings of concern to us. The more specific and technical meaning will be discussed in Chapter 4. For the present, we will use *finish* in the more general sense as it is used by the public all of the time and by the refinisher some of the time.

When someone speaks of a beautiful finish on a piece of furniture he is talking about the total effect created by all the things that were done to the raw wood to bring it to its final appearance. He is not speaking of any one of the several processes that were applied to the piece but of all of them. The finish, then, is everything that was done to the wood to make the piece ready to use.

To *re*finish is to remove an old finish down to the original bare wood and follow this with the application of an entirely new finish. The removal of an old finish is a procedure that consists of one or more steps or processes. The application of a new finish usually requires several distinct processes. Information for making intelligent choices about these processes and directions for executing them constitute the bulk of this volume.

To *restore* a finish is to repair an existing finish, to bring it back to its original state. Restoring does *not* include the removal of the old finish. In restoring a finish one uses many of the processes of applying a new finish except that some of the techniques are altered to fit the situation. The techniques particularly applicable to restoring will be discussed in Chapter 13.

Finishing a piece of furniture is the application of a finish to the raw wood of a newly constructed piece. The processes required are the same as those that follow the removal of an old finish when refinishing a piece. Since finishing as an independent procedure will not be discussed later, we will consider one further detail here.

A great deal of "unfinished furniture" is sold today. This means, of course, that no finish has been applied to the raw wood. Most buyers fail to realize that the construction is unfinished also. These pieces must be sanded.

We have said and will repeat that sandpaper is not to be used in refinishing or finishing. In this case, however, we are completing the construction before beginning the finishing. So get out the sandpaper and get the piece smooth. Power sanders are still taboo except in very skilled hands. Light hand-sanding is all that is normally required.

When the construction is completed and all sandpaper thrown away, you are ready to apply the finish. From this point on, the piece is regarded as though it has just been stripped. Instructions for selecting and applying the finish are found in subsequent chapters.

Restore or Refinish?

Now we come to the final important point in this chapter: restore or refinish? This problem can become a real sticky wicket but, before considering it directly, there is a common psychological problem that should be overcome.

For some unknown reason the great majority of people seem to feel that every old piece of furniture should be stripped of its finish, right down to the bare wood, and then finished in its natural color. To be sure, some of these folk want to change the color with a little stain, but the basic drive appears to be: Strip It Bare and Apply a New Finish. If you have a psychological block against restoring, consider carefully why you should change your attitude—money and effort!

The money factor applies to old and antique pieces, the condition of which, obviously, should be as original as is feasible. When the remaining original finish is of such quality and condition that it can be *well* restored, this should be done in order to maintain the beauty and value of the piece. Failure to do so could result in a financial loss of 25 to 75 percent of the potential value.

The second reason for restoring rather than refinishing applies to any furniture, the near new as well as the old and antique: A complete refinishing job is *hard work*. It is hard physical labor even if it is done correctly by following the instructions in subsequent chapters. We have found few people who would knowingly choose the more difficult path. Now, with two such excellent reasons for restoring when possible, if you have a hangup about bare wood, you should be able to get rid of it.

The refinisher, amateur or professional, is faced often with deciding whether a piece should be restored or completely refinished. While most pieces fall readily into one category or the other, many do not. If little or none of the original finish remains or if large areas are badly damaged, the piece will have to be refinished. This is also the case when the original finish has been covered with layers of paint or unknown junk. If the original finish is largely intact, though dulled with age or years of wax and polish, even if there is minor damage due to normal wear or slight mistreatment, the piece should definitely be restored rather than refinished. (Of course, when a customer wants a cherry table to become walnut, one must refinish regardless of condition!) However, nothing is as simple as at first it seems.

When all is said and done, a large number of borderline pieces remain as candidates for both restoring and refinishing. Only on the basis of personal experience can the refinisher make this decision knowing that he will *usually* be right. We can, however, give you a few guidelines and a few specifics to help you while you gain the experience relatively painlessly. The specifics are presented in Chapter 13; the guidelines, here.

1. Restore and, thereby, preserve an original finish on an antique if it is practical to do so. Keeping the original finish, even if restored, will enhance the value of an antique.
2. While there is no financial advantage, the finish on new or simply old furniture or on an antique that has been refinished previously should be restored if possible. There is a decided time and energy advantage in restoring *any* finish.

3. If you suspect that a piece has a restorable finish, give it a try. At first you may be wrong often, but it is worth a try, since little time and effort are usually required to find out. Even when you are wrong, you will be gaining restoring skills. There is very little to be lost, and there will be some very pleasant surprises in the course of time. If restoring doesn't work out, no harm has been done—just refinish.
4. Every type of finish—varnish, shellac, lacquer, enamel, flat paint, and oil —may be restored if its condition is suitable.
5. Most physical problems from which furniture suffers do not, in themselves, preclude restoration of a finish. The repairing of loose joints, tack and nail holes, gouges, and the like interferes no more with restoring than with refinishing.

There is one final point to be made about restoring. As in every line of work, there are all kinds of commercial refinishers. Some will do each job very well. Many will charge a reasonable price for the job they do. Most are, in broad terms, honest. Some, however, will take you for all they can, and one of the tricks these birds like best is to charge a bare-wood price for a quick restoring job. Such an operator can spot an unwary and uninformed owner three blocks away, and he charges accordingly. It is not unusual for him to charge $50 to $75 or even more for a $5 or $10 job. He does this by using techniques in this book, especially those in Chapter 13. The moral is obvious.

3

Woods

The home refinisher should be aware that furniture has been made from every conceivable type of wood from the most common to the most exotic. Most furniture makers choose the most readily obtainable wood that has characteristics suitable for the piece. Often, that which is at hand was (and is) chosen with little regard for color, grain, hardness, or strength. However, most requirements can be met with six basic woods. The great majority of furniture is made of cherry, mahogany, maple, oak, pine, and walnut.

Identifying Woods—or Learning to Identify Woods

The uninformed seem to believe that the identification of wood is a simple matter that could easily be mastered if only someone would provide the key. It is true that trees are easily identified by their leaves, flowers, fruit, bark, branching, and other obvious characteristics. Despite this fact, when a tree is cut into boards, the identification may be extremely difficult. Each wood does have a typical grain. With a little homework it is possible to glance at some types of wood and know immediately what they are.

Complicating Factors in Identification

Identification complications are caused by three major factors. The first and most obvious problem in furniture is that the grain may be completely hidden by paint or other opaque finishes. When the grain is visible it is often obscured by stain and finish. The stain remaining in a stripped but unbleached piece continues to make the grain indistinct. Color is obviously of little value in identification because of previous staining and natural variability.

The second complication is that boards may be cut from trees in various ways. This greatly affects the appearance of the grain pattern. It often happens that a board will display a pattern that is quite different from the typical one.

TWO METHODS OF SAWING LUMBER

PLAIN SAWED   QUARTER SAWED

The third complication is caused by the fact that trees grow in different locations under different conditions. Climate of the growing area (general temperature, availability of water and sunlight) and the presence or absence of various minerals can greatly affect the appearance of wood.

Finally, there are often many subtypes (species) of trees that are called by the same general name. For example, there are four *major* types of birch, five of mahogany, eleven of oak, and fifteen of pine.

The result of these complications is that while an experienced person can sometimes say, "That piece is walnut," he should, in all honesty, say, "That is *probably* walnut." It is interesting to see two informed dealers argue vehemently over the type of wood in a piece. They finally agree that either could be right, that both could be wrong, and that it really does not matter anyway. Don't be taken in by the fellow who takes his knife to scrape off a bit of finish to identify the wood. This test is anything but conclusive in identifying wood.

What all of this means to the refinisher, amateur or professional, is that a piece can be refinished to look like any of several kinds of wood unless the grain is quite distinctive. Even oak, which usually has an easily identifiable grain, can often be finished to look like walnut. Undoubtedly, we have all admired beautiful "cherry" pieces that were actually maple and "walnut" pieces that may have been mahogany or something else.

The point of all of this information about woods is that when a piece is refinished it can be made to look like almost any type of wood. It is desirable to study woods so that you do not end up with a "walnut" table that has an obvious oak grain. Beyond that, it does not matter.

This "faking of woods," as it is called in the trade, sounds a bit like cheating. If you knowingly pass off an oak table for pecan, then that is cheating, especially if it is *sold* under false colors.

The practice of faking wood is so widespread among both manufacturers of new furniture, and refinishers of old furniture, that it is assumed everyone knows about it. It is accepted as legitimate practice. After all, if you have a table that looks, feels, and acts like walnut, what does it matter that it is made of cherry? The trade takes the position that it does not matter unless you pay a premium price for what you don't get.

Characteristics of Woods

The identification of furniture wood can be narrowed somewhat since all are divided into two broad categories. "Hardwoods" are those which come from deciduous, leaf-bearing trees. Generally, they have a grain that varies from close to open, and they are physically hard. These woods are more expensive and, because of their characteristics, have been and are used in the construction of finer furniture.

"Softwoods" are those from coniferous, needle-bearing, evergreen trees. Generally, they have a very open or wide grain and are physically softer than hardwoods. Softwoods are less expensive, readily available, and easier to "work"—i.e., to saw, plane, shape, and so on. They have been and are used in the construction of more rustic types of furniture.

The chart that follows will be of some help to the beginner in preliminary identification of woods. The neophyte should keep in

WOOD	COLOR			GRAIN			HARDNESS			TOOLING	
	light	med.	dark	close	open	wide	low	med.	high	easy	hard
Ash	x	x			x				x	x	x
Cedar	x	x		x				x		x	
Cherry		x	x	x				x		x	x
Fir		x				x	x	x			x
Gum	x	x			x	x	x	x		x	
Mahogany		x	x		x			x	x	x	
Maple		x		x				x		x	
Oak	x	x			x				x	x	x
Pecan		x			x			x		x	
Pine	x				x	x				x	
Poplar	x				x	x	x	x		x	
Redwood		x			x	x	x	x		x	
Rosewood	x	x	x		x			x	x	x	
Satinwood		x	x		x			x	x	x	
Spruce	x	x				x	x			x	
Teak	x	x	x		x			x	x	x	
Walnut		x	x		x			x	x	x	

mind that any given wood can display a variation in characteristics for reasons mentioned earlier. Then, too, only the more commonly used furniture woods are listed. To include all types so used would necessitate the listing of every wood that grows in all parts of the world—a needless as well as impossible task.

In spite of all the variables, one does need a beginning point. The chart is presented as just that—a point of departure for learning to identify woods.

Veneer, Marquetry, Inlay

Often in the construction of furniture the exposed surface of a wood will be covered partially or completely with a thin layer of another wood. This "covering" is called veneer, marquetry, or inlay. We shall use the general term *veneer* for this process and for the product since we are not concerned with the finer distinctions among them.

Veneers have been used on the finest furniture since the fifteenth century. By the eighteenth century they were widely used by skilled cabinetmakers. Three factors have been the basis for the widespread use of veneer over the years—design, decoration, and economics.

Some of the most beautiful pieces of furniture in existence today *required* the use of veneer. Many woods cannot be bent successfully. Often the design of an elegant piece required the bending of wood, sometimes into fairly complex shapes. In cases where this process would damage the appearance of the surface, the obvious solution was to cover that surface with a thin layer that could be bent without cosmetic damage. Had veneering not been possible, most such designs would never have been used.

The use of veneer for decoration is well known. A less expensive wood may be "decorated" with an expensive veneer. An expensive wood may be further improved in appearance through the use of veneers of other types. Then, too, decorative veneers from selected woods and parts of woods simply do not grow in sizes large enough for furniture construction.

Economics is, of course, a third reason for veneering. The veneer is used to conceal the fact that the piece is constructed of a cheap and less desirable type of wood. This use is what has given a bad name to veneered furniture, especially since this is often inferior veneer applied with inferior glue.

The important point here is that there is good veneer and there is poor veneer. The uninitiated frequently believe that all veneered furniture is inferior to solid pieces. This is *not* the case, and the furniture buyer who does not know this will pass up many good pieces over the years. Certainly, one must learn to distinguish between the good and the bad.

The presence of veneer on a piece may be very difficult to detect. It is most easily seen on the edges of flat parts, but even this may require very close examination. Of course, the different appearance of the outer and inner surfaces of a part will usually tell the story.

It should be pointed out here to the beginning refinisher that veneer need not be avoided for supposed difficulties in working with it. As will be seen in subsequent chapters, a veneered piece is treated little, if any, differently from a solid piece. As far as repair is concerned, slightly or even moderately damaged veneer is no more difficult to deal with than is solid wood. Of course, severely damaged veneer or solid wood may be another matter.

The identification of veneers is often even more difficult than of solid wood. The base wood is less open to inspection and may be hard to name for this reason alone. As for the veneer itself, identification is complicated beyond solid wood by the fact that it is cut in a variety of ways.

Basically, veneer is produced from a log in one of two ways. It may be "cut" by sawing or slicing the log lengthwise, or it may be "peeled" by slicing around the log. It is obvious that the pattern of the grain in the veneer of a single type of wood can differ substantially, depending on whether it has been cut or peeled.

TWO METHODS OF SAWING VENEER

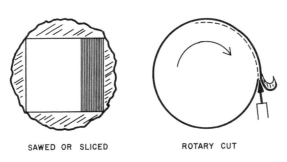

SAWED OR SLICED   ROTARY CUT

Summary

There are many complex and complicating factors in wood identification. *Positive* identification of the wood in a piece of furniture is frequently very difficult and may be impossible. There are very few true experts in this field in spite of the large number who have this (usually local) reputation.

Sometimes it seems that the only way to be sure is to cut the tree, saw and cure the lumber, and then build the piece! Fortunately, it is not actually that bad. In many instances identification is quick and sure. In more obscure cases absolute identification is unnecessary and unimportant.

As far as the wood, only, is concerned, there are two important questions. First, *Is the nature of the wood suitable to the design and function of the piece?* Second, *Since this wood is not obviously identifiable, what kind do I want it to look like after it is refinished?* We suggest that you consider these important things and let the experts, real and so called, argue over the obscurities.

4

Choosing the Type of Finish

Just as there is a fixed sequence to the various processes used in refinishing a piece of furniture, so there is a sequence to the decisions the refinisher must make. Most of these decisions may be made along the way as the piece proceeds through the processes. We shall defer discussion of those decisions until we reach the point where each must be made. There are others that must be made at times that are apparently out of synchronization with the refinishing processes. The most important of these concerns the type of finish that ultimately will be applied.

It is necessary at this time to digress slightly in order to complete our discussion of the meanings of the word *finish* that was begun in Chapter 2. *Finish* is commonly used to mean all those things that have been done to the surface of a piece to give it its final appearance. Finishers and refinishers frequently use the term in a more specialized way. This more specific meaning must be used for the first time in this chapter.

Generally, raw wood has a number of things done to it in order to make the piece of furniture ready to use. These may be put into several groups: preparing the surface, applying color, applying a protective coating, and applying a final dressing. Finishing *(general)* is all of these things. Finishing *(specific)* is only the application of a protective coating. The protective coating may be varnish, paint, oil, or various other substances.

It is advantageous to decide on the type of finish (protective coating) that is to be used before the refinishing or finishing processes are begun. Failure to do so will sometimes result in extra work for the refinisher and may cause alteration of the surface to such an extent that some types of finish can no longer be used. This does not mean that the decision cannot be made after the processes are begun. Indeed, the decision can be made right up to the moment that a finish is applied, but the further the piece has moved through the processes, the narrower the *range* of possibilities becomes. The reasons for this fact will become apparent as the discussion progresses, but, for now, the type of finish should be decided on right at the beginning.

This decision can be made effectively only with adequate information about the characteristics of the various finishes. The remainder of this chapter includes a discussion of the advantages and disadvantages of each type of finish. Also included is a unique chart, "Refinisher's Pathfinder," which leads through the processes themselves.

Every finish may be classified as either opaque or clear. An opaque finish is one of several types of paint. Wood grain, even the wood itself, cannot be seen through an opaque finish. Judging by appearances, a piece of furniture with a paint finish could be constructed of wood or metal or plastic or any solid material. Paint is used on furniture either to hide the material of which it is made or to create special effects. An old or antique piece should be painted only if its *original* finish was paint, and even then it may be finished clear.

Clear finishes are often called "natural wood" finishes, though it is obvious that the wood showing through may be, and usually is, anything but "natural." Clear finishes are those protective coatings through which the wood and its grain may be seen. We classify clear finishes as soft, hard, or oil. Sealer and so-called "wax" finishes are soft. Varnish, shellac, and lacquer finishes are hard. Each of these will be considered separately.

Now, let us take a look at the paint finishes. By and large, most furniture painting is done by those who would rather do otherwise, but they do not know how to get a *good* clear finish. They rush to the paint store where, after choosing a nonwood color, they select a can of flat paint or enamel. Flat or enamel, the only significant difference is that the enamel is glossy or shiny to some specified degree. While we must admit that this so-called refinishing is the easiest to accomplish, these misguided folk have for their effort only a utilitarian piece with no intrinsic beauty of its own.

Those who choose one of the readily available "antiquing kits" are but slightly better off. Though there are several varieties of such kits with minor variations in technique, the basic idea is to paint the piece with an overall ground color and then apply another color. The second application is supposed to be smeared around to give the appearance of great age and use. The theory may be great, but, in practice, the furniture looks like just what it is—a piece with paint smeared around on it.

We urge you not to waste your time and ruin the appearance of a good piece this way. In the event that you insist, abbreviated instructions are reluctantly given in Chapter 10. We suggest that, at most, you try it on an old packing case. However, take a good look at that old packing case before you splash paint on it. It may be valuable!

There are only two types of paint recommended, and these should be used only on pieces that were originally painted by their builders. One paint is "refinisher's enamel," and the other is milk paint. Both of these are readily obtainable, though neither is available, as such, in a paint store.

Refinisher's enamel looks like regular paint only better. It is all but impossible for the amateur to apply a smooth and blemish-free coat of paint, flat or enamel. Even the professional can rarely do so without resorting to a spray gun. The difficulty arises because enamel, whether of high, medium, or low gloss, cannot be abraded with steel wool or sandpaper after it is dry. The coloring is spread throughout the thickness of the coat, so, if the dry surface is abraded to remove the inevitable brush marks, the objectionable result is immediately obvious. Refinisher's enamel overcomes this difficulty.

A coat of refinisher's enamel is, in reality, two coats. The first is a coat of flat paint, which may be smoothed with steel wool without visual damage. The steel-wooled flat paint is then given a coat of varnish of the desired degree of gloss. The result is what appears to be an unbelievably perfect finish.

The second and final recommendation of paint finishes is milk paint. Early settlers in this country and rural folk for years thereafter used this homemade product to protect and decorate some of their furniture. Though milk paint is certainly not available commercially today, it may be made more easily in home or shop than it could in the days of our ancestors. As the name implies, this paint is made from milk, natural or dehydrated powder or crystal, the latter being far simpler to use. Though the ancients used clay or blood or berries for color, modern packaged colors are more convenient.

Milk paint, ancient or modern, dries to a very hard, almost cementlike coating that is impervious to commercial paint removers. At any rate, purists will certainly want to use it to refinish or restore pieces that originally had this finish.

Detailed instructions on refinisher's enamel and milk paint will be found in Chapter 10. Sufficient information has been presented here to enable the refinisher to decide whether to use an opaque finish and, if so, which one. We shall now consider the clear finishes, which are classified as soft, hard, and oil.

The sealer finish, sometimes called sealer wax or wax finish, is a soft clear finish. It is smooth, dull gloss, and lacking in real or apparent depth. Sealer finish is called soft because it is relatively fragile—that is, it is more easily damaged than other clear finishes. For this reason it is seldom used. Its only advantage is that it is the quickest and easiest of these finishes to apply. The sealer finish is not recommended for pieces that will receive more than minimal usage.

The hard clear finishes are varnish, shellac, and lacquer. They result in an exceptionally smooth, very hard surface that may vary from dull through satin to high gloss. The depth of these finishes varies with the type and number of applications or coats.

Varnish is the finish preferred by quality cabinetmakers and refinishers because it is the hardest finish; it is waterproof and alcohol-proof; and it is most easily given any desired degree of gloss. Varnish is applied more satisfactorily with a brush than by spraying and it takes longer to dry—about twelve hours, depending on the temperature and humidity. This, of course, is why varnish is seldom, if ever, found on mass-produced furniture. Parenthetically, factories use spray lacquer which dries in a few seconds and which, even with several coats on more expensive furniture, does not equal in quality one coat of varnish. One must pay a premium price for furniture with a varnish finish.

Lacquer is the most fragile of the hard finishes, and it has less depth than the others. Since it is also very difficult to apply with a brush, we do not recommend its use by the home refinisher. It is suited to the production line, and that is where it should remain. If, for some reason, the use of lacquer is decided on, it is best applied by spraying. The refinisher should either buy it in spray cans, which becomes quite expensive in larger quantities, or invest $75 or more in a spray outfit of good quality. The secret of success in spraying is practice, practice, and more practice. Spraying an entire piece is quite different from doing a little patchwork spraying when restoring.

The third hard clear finish is shellac, which is of medium hardness between varnish and lacquer. While shellac looks much like varnish, it differs in several important respects. First, it will not react with wax, and so it may be applied to a surface that is not completely wax-free. Second, a coat of shellac is normally somewhat thicker than one of varnish. For this reason, shellac is often used to build up a depth or a body to a finish.

Aside from the fact that it is not quite as hard as varnish, the major disadvantage to shellac is that it is neither waterproof nor alcohol-proof. One or more coats of shellac (and lacquer as well) covered with a good wax dressing can be classified only as water-resistant. This finish is water-resistant only because of the wax, which prevents water from getting to the shellac immediately. Shellac reacts quickly to the presence of water by discoloring—that is, by turning cloudy-white. This quality causes another problem. If shellac is applied in a high-humidity environment—as, for example, on a muggy or rainy day—it is likely to dry with a cloudy or whitish cast rather than clear.

Fortunately, the use of one of these three hard clear finishes does not preclude the use of the others. In fact, shellac and varnish are often used together in order to realize the advantages of both. In such cases, a coat of varnish is applied over a shellac finish; there is no point in putting shellac over varnish. Shellac is used first because of the presence of wax or in order to build body more quickly, and then one coat of varnish is used to provide a finish of additional toughness and one that will not be damaged by water or alcohol.

Having considered the soft and the hard clear finishes, we turn now to the most beautiful of finishes—oil. In spite of its name, the oil finish has no appearance or feeling of oiliness. It is a velvety-smooth finish of medium hardness that is often suited to fine antiques that will not be subjected to hard use. The appearance of an oil finish can be approached but not equaled by a judicious combination of shellac, varnish, and dressing (wax).

Before the development and marketing of certain products that will be discussed in Chapter 11, the application of an oil finish was a back-breaking job that required literally months of effort. If the linseed-oil method were the only one available, we would advise the refinisher to forget the whole thing except in the most extenuating circumstances. Fortunately, one may now choose the unsurpassed beauty of an oil finish, knowing that it is but a little more difficult to achieve than the other types.

The foregoing information on finishes should be sufficient for you to decide which type you wish to use on your project. Even if you are not sure, make a tentative decision now and hold your reservations while you read on.

At this point you, the refinisher, are ready to begin the actual refinishing processes on the basis of the several decisions that have been made. First, you decided that you would do the job yourself. Then you decided which piece of furniture to refinish. Next, you decided on the wood color of the final result. Finally, you have decided on the type of finish to use. Now you are ready to get to work—but how?

The following chapters, constituting Part II of this volume, contain detailed instructions for nine refinishing processes and an uncounted number of variations on each one. Plunging directly into Part II can be quite bewildering to the beginner, who may become confused about which instructions to follow. It is especially for the beginner that the "Refinisher's Pathfinder" has been designed. Old hands at refinishing may choose to ignore the Pathfinder, but even they probably will find it useful.

The main part of the Pathfinder is located on page 29. The types of finishes are listed across the top, and, moving downward from the selected type, the refinisher will find sequential numbers indicating the specified process chapters that apply directly to that finish. Processes (and chapters) marked with an asterisk are those for which the need is determined by the condition of the piece.

Lists have been placed at the beginning of each process chapter. They indicate which sections of their associated chapters are directly applicable to various subprocesses.

To illustrate the use of the Pathfinder, let us suppose that you have decided to put varnish on a small table. Using the main chart here, you would look on the left side and, under Natural Wood Finishes, find the column headed "Hard (Varnish, Shellac, Lacquer)." The four numbers in that column indicate the processes that must be applied to your table and, further, the sequence in which they must be used. The table must be as follows.

REFINISHER'S PATHFINDER

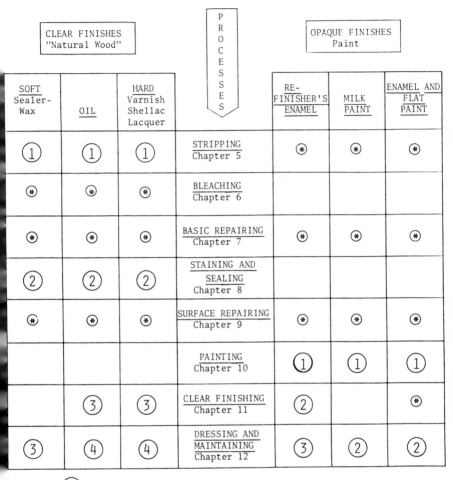

CLEAR FINISHES "Natural Wood"			PROCESSES	OPAQUE FINISHES Paint		
SOFT Sealer-Wax	OIL	HARD Varnish Shellac Lacquer		RE-FINISHER'S ENAMEL	MILK PAINT	ENAMEL AND FLAT PAINT
①	①	①	STRIPPING Chapter 5	✱	✱	✱
✱	✱	✱	BLEACHING Chapter 6			
✱	✱	✱	BASIC REPAIRING Chapter 7	✱	✱	✱
②	②	②	STAINING AND SEALING Chapter 8			
✱	✱	✱	SURFACE REPAIRING Chapter 9	✱	✱	✱
			PAINTING Chapter 10	①	①	①
	③	③	CLEAR FINISHING Chapter 11	②		✱
③	④	④	DRESSING AND MAINTAINING Chapter 12	③	②	②

① Necessary sequential processes
✱ Optional processes

1. Stripped (Chapter 5)
2. Stained and sealed (Chapter 8)
3. Clear-finished (Chapter 11)
4. Dressed and maintained (Chapter 12)

In addition, asterisks in the column point out that the table may have to be bleached (Chapter 6); it may need basic repairs (Chapter 7); and it may need surface repairs (Chapter 9).

The refinisher thus knows in exactly which chapters he must look to find the instructions for refinishing his table. Of course, it will be necessary to read the introductory paragraphs about the optional processes in order to determine whether or not they will be necessary on this particular piece of furniture.

To continue the illustration, the list at the beginning of Chapter 11 indicates which parts of that chapter are applicable to the varnish finish. Thus, you may concentrate on those parts for your table and safely ignore the others having to do with shellac exclusively.

Though the Pathfinder will show you exactly where to find the specific instructions you will need with each piece of furniture, we recommend that you read through every one of the chapters in Part II before beginning the first piece. This should not be done with the idea of learning all the details presented, for that would be a difficult task. Rather, these process chapters should be read to acquire an overall feeling for refinishing from beginning to end. After you have a general understanding, you can follow the Pathfinder and then the specific instructions more easily.

If you are a rank beginner with the very first piece standing before you, do not hesitate to tackle it. There is a double guarantee of ultimate success. First, this book furnishes everything you need except the supplies and the muscle. Second, even if you should do something absolutely wrong, there is no real harm done——just pretend that you acquired the piece in that condition and start over. So there is nothing to lose. Jump in, the water is fine! And good luck to you!

II

The Processes
of Refinishing

5

Stripping

Stripping is the first process in refinishing. It is the removal of the old finish or the several old finishes that may have been applied one over another. At the same time stripping removes the sometimes considerable accumulation of wax and polish and dirt that the years have produced. This process is "stripping" the piece to the bare wood in order that a new finish may be subsequently applied. Stripping is always done if the new finish is to be one of the clear (natural wood) types. If the new finish is to be one of the opaque (paint) types, the piece *may* be stripped, but this process is usually unnecessary.

When a piece is to be painted, stripping for the purpose of exposing the wood grain is a complete waste of time and effort. As will be discussed at the beginning of Chapter 10, the basic preparation of a surface for painting is to smooth it evenly. There are times when stripping is the best method of achieving a smooth surface. For example, a piece may have a thick covering of several layers of paint. Cracks and chips in this covering may be filled, but often the best solution is to strip the old paint from the piece altogether.

You have made all the decisions that were discussed in Part I of this book, and your first project stands before you ready to be stripped. At this point we urge you to take one more critical look at the piece, keeping in mind the contents of Chapters 2 and 13. If the finish can be well restored, that should be done in order to save time and work.

Finish Removers (Strippers)

Problems will be encountered in stripping, to say the least. Our intention is not to discourage you but to give you fair warning that we use no magic. This process is hard work, and it takes a great amount of patience at times. Stripping has never been described as a fun thing, but the rewards are more than worth all the trouble. In order to avoid as much trouble as possible, the instructions that follow will guide the beginner step by step through the stripping process. At the same time, the experienced refinisher will be provided with improved methods and techniques.

SANDPAPER

One of the ground rules (and there are a few) is that sandpaper must be eliminated from your stock of materials. Absolutely no sanding should be done on old furniture. Sandpaper is fine for such things as floors and woodwork. We even recommend it for a few specific uses but not in the stripping operation. There is an excellent reason for not using sandpaper to remove an old finish.

A flawless mirrorlike surface can be obtained by using sandpaper. If this is desired, it is much easier to go out and buy a reproduction. If you want a smooth, mellow, aged, velvety-looking finish, forget the sandpaper. That old soft appearance is called *patina*. Patina is caused by years and years of use, resulting in the action of light and air on the wood and in countless minute dents and scratches. It takes years for a piece of furniture to acquire patina but only a few minutes to destroy it with sandpaper. As we proceed, you will soon learn a better, easier, and faster way—one that will not harm the patina or the wood in any way. So forget that sandpaper is even available, and you will soon reach the point that it is insulting when someone asks if you sanded a particular piece.

COMMERCIAL TANKS

There are several methods of stripping an old piece. One, which we obviously do *not* recommend, is sandpaper. Another method is one about which this refinisher has serious reservations. It is used by several highly advertised chains that specialize in stripping—not refinishing but simply stripping furniture.

These folk remove finishes in a matter of minutes by dipping the piece in a tank or vat of remover. While this is not practical for a large piece such as a piano, it could be very advantageous with smaller pieces. If it is worth the fee and you can overcome the transportation problems that may be involved, you may wish to try it. Even so, we advise that you proceed with caution, for the results greatly depend on the solutions used, the knowledge and skill of the operator, and the piece itself. Watch for sign stating "Not responsible for glue, veneer, et cetera."

To realize what can happen, consider the case of a lovely old washstand which was taken for this commercial stripping. The piece was dipped and the old finish fairly flew off. Unfortunately the remover also affected the glue, and the washstand came completely apart. In this instance the glue and the solution were incompatible. Certainly this does not happen often. One does not always need a large bag to take home the parts.

In the hands of a competent operator these commercial stripping processes do a good job. It is the side effects that make careful consideration necessary. Their successful jobs often result in badly raised wood fibers. Before entrusting even mediocre pieces to an unknown process, at least inspect carefully some samples of its results.

We do recommend a method of stripping that is both foolproof and relatively easy. We use a solution packaged in a can with a label that specifies: LIQUID NO-WASH PAINT AND VARNISH REMOVER. This remover works equally well on paint, varnish, shellac, and lacquer but does not affect glue when used as directed. The name in itself says a lot about this remover. It is by far the most practical and has made refinishers out of many who wouldn't attempt the job with the wash-off and other types mentioned later.

The many varieties of strippers available come under the label of paint and varnish removers. Most will do just that. Some are better, others better *and* cheaper, and there are a few that are just more expensive. We could go into great detail, but our goal is to inform you of a few types and show you the path that our years of experience have finally cleared.

The remover recommended is the most practical type. It enables one to strip old finishes indoors or out. Neither normal dampness, heat, nor cold have any effect on it. It does not change the color of the wood, as other methods frequently do. One of two inexpensive removers should be asked for by brand name: KWIK LIQUID NO WASH or KUTZIT PAINT REMOVER. We prefer Kwik, but Kutzit is a close second choice. Merchants in your area will surely carry one or the other of these. There are more expensive brands, but all that we have tried did the job no better and sometimes not as well, especially on the clear hard finishes. The salesman may recommend another brand, especially if he has neither Kwik nor Kutzit, but find out how much refinishing he has actually done before taking his word. Our third choice is so inferior to these two that we never use it.

The liquid no-wash is excellent for beginners as well as the more experienced. Not only is it very effective in stripping, but it has the great advantage that it does not have to be neutralized with another chemical nor washed off with water. Many refinishing shops use the liquid no-wash. There is less waiting time between stripping and the next process than there is with other methods. This remover penetrates little more than the old finish, and, therefore, the time allowed for drying is minimized, especially since no water is used. The unused portion stores very well for later use. For removing exceptionally stubborn finishes, a heavy-duty no-wash is also available. We will return to specific directions shortly.

WARNING

Many of the products used in refinishing are highly flammable and must not be used near open flames. Even smoking should be limited to other areas when they are in use. These products also produce vapors that are harmful if inhaled in high concentration. When these products, such as both of the paint and varnish removers mentioned, are used indoors it is essential that windows be opened. An exhaust fan is a sure way to eliminate possible harm from the vapors, and turning on the fan should always be the first step if you work indoors.

WASH-OFF REMOVERS

The wash-off type removers are still available. Almost all manufacturers in the paint business have their brand on the store shelves. These vary from thin liquids to thick pastes. There is absolutely nothing wrong with the wash-off removers. The real disadvantage is the limitation of their use. We emphasize the advantage of working indoors, and it is very difficult, if not impossible, to use a wash-off remover indoors. The wash-off remover is just that: You need a garden hose and plenty of water. That, in turn, takes more drying time after the piece has been saturated with remover and water. These removers, too, will not change the color of the wood. If you do use a wash-off remover, read the labels carefully, as we advise with every product.

LYE

With so many good removers readily available, it seems rather a waste of time to mention others, but no refinisher should lack at least a passing knowledge of them.

Lye was the favored paint remover for many years, but it must have been so because nothing else was available. The disadvantages are many and the advantages few, if any. Lye is very difficult to work with, unkind to skin, and, unless great care is taken, downright unfriendly to wood. It must be used outdoors with a garden hose handy and in the sunshine. It should not be used on grass unless you are trying to kill it. The lye bath is used as a last resort by the home refinisher and then only on paint. It is too harsh for any but the very heaviest coatings of varnish, shellac, or lacquer. If you must try it, follow the instructions below carefully.

Skin and eyes must be well protected. Long sleeves, gloves, and safety goggles are essential. Lye is purchased in dry form at a grocery store and must be mixed with water. A thirteen-ounce can is poured *slowly* into a quart of water. (Do *not* pour water into a container of lye. This is likely to cause a vigorous chemical reaction resulting in great sputtering and splashing and corresponding hazard to surroundings—including you.) These precautions cannot be overemphasized.

Outside on a warm day and in the sunshine, the lye solution is applied with a long-handled mop to the entire painted surface. The paint will begin to soften in a couple of minutes. The lye must not be left on too long or it will damage the wood. As soon as the paint has softened, the piece must be sprayed with the water hose and the paint scrubbed off with a stiff brush. Working quickly, you scrub the piece with straight vinegar, which stops the action of the lye. The vinegar must get down into every little crevice. The piece is rinsed again with the hose and then dried as much as possible with old cloths. Since this procedure frequently darkens the wood, the piece must now be bleached (see Chapter 6). Four or five days must be allowed for drying. All of this moisture has raised the wood fibers so that the surfaces are fuzzy and must be smoothed with grade-2 steel wool.

Even the beginner can easily see that the lye treatment is a traumatic experience for any piece of furniture. It could be complete disaster for a fine antique. The entire lye operation must be approached with great caution.

SODA-AMMONIA

There is a home-made stripper that is not as well known as lye. This soda-ammonia remover is much safer than lye for both the refinisher and the wood. It will not burn wood or skin, though it will kill grass. It is quite cheap to make and is fairly effective on clear finishes. Soda-ammonia remover does not work so well on most types of paint.

As the name implies, this stripper is made of *washing soda* and regular household *ammonia.* You simply mix these chemicals to the consistency of a watery paste, but this is not as easy as it sounds. The washing soda is difficult to dissolve in ammonia. If you plan to use only a small amount, you can put some soda into a plastic bowl, pour in some ammonia, and stir it around a bit. Pour off the liquid remover, leaving the undissolved lumps of soda in the bowl. For larger quantities you can try one of three approaches: Locate some powdered washing soda, or grind into powder the granular soda, or dissolve the soda in a small quantity of warm water before mixing in the ammonia. Don't mix too much at once because it won't keep. Be sure that you are using *washing* soda—not *baking* soda.

Once mixed, soda-ammonia stripper is easy to use. Just put it on the surface with a brush, a sponge, or a cloth. Apply it generously. You may want to rub the wet surface with 3/0 steel wool to help loosen the old finish. *Before the stripper dries,* wash it and the loose finish off with running water. Wipe off the water with cloths and let the wood dry. Repeat as necessary.

Soda-ammonia remover is not as effective as Kwik, and it leaves the wood wet with water like the commercial wash-off removers. You may wish to use it when expense rather than time is the most important consideration.

There are other types of removers, but they suffer from various combinations of the disadvantages of the wash-offs, lye, and soda-ammonia. In addition they are less effective. We will dispense with the grizzly details and settle on the liquid no-wash removers.

Other Supplies

As indicated earlier, the work space can be anywhere. A spare corner of a den, an unused bedroom, or, of course, a garage or basement are excellent places. This does not mean that you must work indoors; all of the following directions can be used for outdoor work as well. We emphasize the indoor method because of its practicability. One can't easily move a piano in and out, and many a large piece is unrefinished because it could not be left outdoors for weeks while being refinished. It can be stripped where it stands. This is possible without wrecking the entire house!

You have already chosen the piece on which you will work. If it is your first project, the piece is small and plain with little carving or other ornamentation. It also has a hard, clear finish, since that is generally easier to strip than is paint.

It is time to make a list of needed supplies. The initial outlay can be less than $15, but, if you are not careful, it can be as much as $25 or more. A gallon of one of the recommended removers sells for about $4, while others go up as high as $12 per gallon. When possible, purchase supplies at the larger discount stores where a good selection of products is usually available at substantial savings.

The listed supplies will be sufficient for several projects, but it is impractical to buy smaller quantities. You will need:

2 inexpensive (cheap) paintbrushes (2" or 2½")
1 putty knife
1 gallon remover (Kwik or Kutzit)
1 box steel wool, grade 1
1 box steel wool, grade 2
1 scrub brush, small, nylon bristles
1 package plastic gloves, disposable

The last item, disposable gloves, may be found in the cosmetic department of a drugstore. We prefer these over the rubber dishwashing type, as they are less bulky and bunglesome.

There are a few more readily available items to assemble, and these can be found around the house. They are:

a discarded toothbrush
a stack of old newspapers
a sheet of plastic (discarded shower curtain)
many rags, about 10" square (from towels, sheets, spreads)
two small cans or jars with wide tops
a large plastic trash or garden bag
old clothes (to wear)
a hair band (for long-haired ladies or men)

Stripping Instructions

The first task is to prepare the work area. These directions are for working indoors, as we said, but modification for outdoor work areas will be readily apparent. Always begin each work session by installing the exhaust fan in the window and turning it on. The floor is protected from spills and spatters by covering it with the plastic sheet. The sheet, in turn, is covered with a layer of newspapers, which greatly simplifies the clean-up process. Minor spills, drops of remover (later stain, finish, etc.), steel-wool particles, and the like can be covered quickly with another layer of newspapers to keep from stepping in and tracking this mess all over the house. For a real clean-up, the newspapers are rolled up and put into the large plastic bag. One further precaution: If you tend to be a little careless or sloppy, anything and everything nearby should be covered to avoid damage from splattered remover or other liquids. Nine- by twelve-foot plastic sheets are excellent for this purpose and may be obtained inexpensively from most paint and hardware stores. Appropriately enough, they are called drop cloths.

As you get into refinishing you will discover that steel wool is the most expensive item used. In order to get the most out of it, we suggest that each pad be unrolled and torn into smaller pieces. The grades 1 and 2 that are used in stripping will be about the right size if each pad is torn into two pieces. Finer steel wool used in subsequent processes will yield more work pieces per pad.

Unless one's hands are quite tough, gloves should always be worn when using steel wool. The minute particles of steel have a way of working into the skin, and they can cause infections if not removed promptly and properly. When using the disposable gloves for this purpose, two or three on each hand will provide added protection.

Now, the piece to be stripped is placed on the newspapers, and all removable parts should be removed—knobs, drawers, doors, mirrors, glass, anything that will come off except the legs! If it is not practical to remove glass or mirrors, they should be protected as much as possible with newspapers and masking tape. The specified removers will not harm them, but it is difficult to clean the remover from them. Removing glass and mirrors eliminates the danger of breakage. Store them in a safe place until ready to reinstall.

No repairs need be made at this point, but the piece should be checked for damage so that you can avoid making it worse during stripping. A split leg or a section of loose veneer, for example, would have to receive special care. A good sturdy table can take vigorous rubbing with steel wool, but a damaged or fragile piece requires more gentle treatment. If a piece, such as a table, is already apart, the job will go faster if stripped as is. (It is reassembled after stripping.) You will find that the smaller parts are easier to work with when separated. A door of a bookcase, for instance, stands a good chance of being damaged at the hinges if it isn't removed and stripped separately. (A small compartmented plastic box is very handy for storing all screws, brass pieces, hinges, and the like until time for replacement.)

Gloves should be worn whenever remover is handled. Some removers are more dangerous than others. Those recommended will not burn the skin like acid and lye, but they can cause skin irritation if left on for a time. It is really quite easy to work with the disposable gloves—not like the more bulky gloves used for cleaning. A clean pair next to the skin is most convenient. If the phone rings, just shed the dirty outer gloves and be on your way.

A very important habit to develop is to work always facing the exhaust fan. In other words, keep the remover and the project between you and the fan. This guarantees that the vapors will be moving away from you.

Before opening the remover read the label carefully. This should always be done with every product used in stripping and finishing furniture. With the fan providing good ventilation, about a cupful of remover is poured into each of the two small cans or jars, which are then capped. Tops should always be kept on containers of remover when they are not being used. First, this cuts down on the amount of vapor released, and, second, it prevents rather rapid loss through evaporation.

One container should be used with a brush to apply the first coat of remover. It will become very dirty rapidly. As the remover is used up, wipe the container occasionally with a rag before refilling. The second container and brush are used for the subsequent applications of remover. This eliminates adding color to the piece, as will happen if very dirty remover is reapplied. Don't dispose of dirty remover, just cap it for use in the first application on the next surface.

Holding a small container of remover near the top of the piece, brush a generous coat on a small area—the top, side, or drawer front —*not* the entire piece. If possible, the piece should be turned so that the surface on which you are working is horizontal, using newspapers to protect other surfaces. Traces of the old finish will be seen on the brush almost immediately, but remover should be brushed on until the binding of the old finish begins to dissolve completely. This will usually require two generous applications of remover following one another immediately so that the surface does not dry between them. Remover that drips or runs onto other surfaces should be wiped off right away.

After five or six minutes much of the dissolved finish can be wiped off with a rag. If the old finish is very thick, it may be pushed off the surface gently with a putty knife which has had its corners and edges filed round in order to prevent gouging or scratching the wood. A third container with a wire stretched across the top is sometimes used with the putty knife. The sludge picked up by the knife falls into the container when it is scraped across the wire. Since the problem then arises of what to do with the sludge in the can, it seems more practical simply to dump the sludge off the putty knife on a piece of newspaper.

No attempt should be made to scrape away the old finish with the putty knife or any other tool. Any remaining finish (and there will be some) will be picked up with subsequent applications of remover. This will do the job for you and completely eliminate the possibility of gouging or scratching the surface.

Directions with many removers recommend using steel wool to work the remover into the old finish in order to speed up the process. We have found this process completely unnecessary with Kwik or Kutzit on varnish, shellac, and lacquer finishes. In addition, the steel wool quickly gets clogged with sludge, and the entire process is too messy. We let the remover do the work. The simplest procedure is to apply a generous coating of remover, wait about five minutes, push off the sludge with a putty knife, wipe away the excess with rags, and immediately rub with grade-2 steel wool to loosen and remove more old finish (grade 1 if the remaining finish is thin).

The first application of remover rarely takes off all of the old finish, so the entire procedure should be repeated as many times as necessary. Twice will be sufficient in most cases. After wiping each application of remover, the use of steel wool immediately will clean more of the old finish.

Steel wool is applied vigorously, always rubbed in the direction of the grain of the wood—*never* across the grain. Great care should be exercised with veneer, especially around the edges, so the steel wooling of veneer must be done more gently. A thick piece of veneer can be rubbed as vigorously as solid wood, but be very careful of the direction. Burled veneer takes some detective work to determine the direction of the grain in the wood. The best insurance is to use grade-0 steel wool, and if damage is done, it will be very slight. In many instances, the finish will have been applied very sparingly on veneer, and no steel wool is needed because the remover will clean it adequately.

A new pad of steel wool should be used whenever needed. You will know when to replace the old one because it will gradually become ineffective. For hard-to-reach areas, the steel wool may be shaped easily as needed. For example, it may be rolled into a rope shape, twisted for strength, and pulled back and forth on areas such as spooling and where legs are attached. Sometimes it is easier to put two pads together to fit around a table or chair leg and rub it back and forth. Use steel wool vigorously on the end grain. This part soaks more stain than other surfaces and often needs special attention.

When the bulk of the old finish has been removed to expose the bare wood, the dirty remover from the number-one can should no longer be used. It may require two or even three applications to reach this stage. Continuing to use the dirty remover will simply put the mess back on as fast as it comes off. The container should be capped and the brush placed in a plastic bag in order to save them for initial use on the next surface.

The second container of clean remover and the fresh brush should be used to clean up the last of the old finish. Usually this will remove the unevenness of color that has been apparent from the beginning. Occasionally, there will be dark or light spots caused by water damage or other mistreatment of the piece. Remover will not eliminate them. Instructions for removing these will be found in the special problems section at the end of this chapter.

There are two general approaches to the removal process. As pointed out earlier, remover should be applied to only one surface at a time. Beyond this the refinisher has a choice: Either each surface of the piece can be stripped *completely* before the next is begun or the entire piece (one surface at a time) can be half cleaned with the number-one container of stripper before the final cleaning is done. There are advantages to each method, and the choice is a matter of individual preference.

If one part at a time is completely cleaned, the piece will not have to be moved and turned so often. This method is psychologically advantageous in that even one completely cleaned surface can motivate the refinisher to get on with the job quickly. The disadvantage is that drips and runs onto a cleaned surface are troublesome since they may cause discoloration with sludge even when promptly wiped away.

Conversely, the half-cleaned all-over method reduces the run problem, though it does require more movement of the piece. The refinisher, particularly the beginner, cannot see as much accomplishment as soon. But take your choice; both approaches work well.

It is not necessary to try to remove all of the old stain unless you wish to make it a lighter color. Some stain will come up with the old finish, but removing stain is accomplished by bleaching (Chapter 6). To prepare the piece for a new finish, it is necessary to remove the old finish (paint, lacquer, or what have you), *not* to remove the old stain. You will readily see when there is only color left; the wood will be smooth, with no rough or dark spots of residue.

The stripping process must be continued over the entire piece, inside drawers, under table tops, and without overlooking knobs, doors, and other parts that have been taken off. You need have no concern if you are interrupted at any time in this procedure. You can answer the telephone that rings just when a coat of remover has been applied. The remover will dry, but another coat will quickly put you back in business with no damage done. (This is not recommended for heavy-duty removers.) The small containers should be closed when not in use, and if the brushes are kept in plastic bags, they can be used for months.

Used newspapers and rags should be kept in a large plastic bag, which should be kept closed. The bag must always be placed outdoors at night. Replace dirty papers under the piece as needed.

You will occasionally have a piece of furniture with carvings or spooling that just cannot be reached with steel wool. In such cases when even the rope of steel wool isn't adequate, we resort to using an old toothbrush. If the toothbrush is not successful, we use a small scrub brush with nylon bristles and a brass bristled brush as a last resort. The brass brush must be used very, very gently because softer wood fibers are broken easily and the end result may be a clean piece of carving that is fuzzy with broken fibers.

Do not be concerned about the darker shade in the spool crevices of legs other than to be certain that no old finish remains. You will notice on many table and chair legs of the spooled variety that the crevices are usually somewhat darker. This is not only acceptable but attractive.

When all of the old finish has been removed, particles of steel wool are left all over the piece. Needless to say, you can't leave any of this around, and a vacuum cleaner is the most desirable way to remove it. Every steel particle must be removed from screw holes, drawers, corners, and crevices. Judicious use of a cloth, a brush, *and* a vacuum cleaner is the only sure way to remove every trace of steel wool and dust. A thorough cleaning is essential. Imagine the problems a hole full of steel-wool particles can cause when you are varnishing, for example, and they fall out on the wet new finish when the piece is turned.

The refinisher who has followed the preceding directions will find the result is a well-stripped piece of furniture about 90 percent of the time. In the other cases there will be conditions that require further, special attention. These are discussed in the following section.

Special Problems

Black Rings   Disfiguring black marks, usually in the form of rings, are often found on the tops of old pieces. They were caused by moisture getting down into the wood itself. Stripper will not take them out effectively. The best way to remove these black rings is to use the bleaching process as explained in Chapter 6. Bleaching must be done after stripping but before staining/sealing.

Brass Parts   See METAL PARTS.

Color in Wood Pores   Normally, paint is quite easy to remove, but it can sometimes cause a serious problem on wood with large pores such as oak. Color pigments can penetrate so far into the pores that remover and steel wool will not pull it out. This can be a very difficult situation.

If you end up with specks of paint pigment down in the pores, try using the nylon brush. Flow on a generous quantity of clean stripper and brush vigorously. If this fails, switch to the brush with fine brass bristles. As a final resort, the brass brush has always done the job for us. Fortunately, such extreme cases are quite rare. We hope you never find one.

Dark Stain　　If the stain that remains after stripping is too dark for the desired final appearance, the piece must be bleached. See Chapter 6.

Dark Wood　　Occasionally, one desires to refinish a piece in a lighter shade than the wood of which it is made. The process of bleaching wood is different from that for bleaching stains. This, too, is included in Chapter 6.

Dry Sinks　　See TIN.

End Grain　　The end grain of wood always absorbs stain more readily than other surfaces. Special attention is always given to these areas in stripping as well as finishing. Many refinishers simply use sandpaper because remover and steel wool just aren't adequate. Sanding the end grain endangers the surrounding areas, especially the top, so this really isn't advisable. The best thing is to bleach the end grain, but this too endangers surrounding areas. Successful bleaching of end grain requires very careful work.

There are two preferred methods of handling dark end grain. The first is to get it as light as possible with remover and leave it as is. Often the darker end grain adds an attractiveness to the refinished piece. The second method is to compensate for the darker ends when restaining the piece. This procedure is discussed in Chapter 8.

Iceboxes　　See METAL PARTS and TIN.

Ink Spots　　Ink and inklike spots are treated as black rings, above.

Metal Parts　　The recommended removers will not harm metal. Usually, metal parts (hinges, knobs, escutcheons, drawer pulls) are taken off the piece. This makes it easier to clean them and the wood. A little remover will take care of any paint, varnish, or the like but will do nothing about rust. Small parts can be cleaned and shined with steel wool. Household ammonia cleans and shines brass beautifully. For larger metal parts, see TIN, below.

Milk Paint   By chance you may encounter an old paint that removers will not touch. It may be the only finish on a piece or it may be covered by other finishes. In fact, this paint is usually discovered when it is exposed after stripper has whisked away covering layers of paint or shellac.

For a time in some parts of the country a paint was made with milk and is called, appropriately, "milk paint." This paint dries to a very hard finish that is extremely resistant to strippers. Since original milk paint has potential value in its own right, careful consideration should be given to restoring it (Chapter 13). If it is not worth restoring, it may be removed quite easily.

Plain household ammonia as found in grocery stores will remove milk paint. It is applied liberally and the sludge is removed in the usual way. The surface must be rinsed well with water. The piece will usually require bleaching, since the ammonia tends to darken wood. There are several precautions that *must* be observed when using ammonia.

Ammonia is very volatile and its fumes are very strong. A well-ventilated area is essential. Ammonia also reacts quite strongly with many other chemicals, so the surface must be free of stripper before ammonia is applied. It dissolves some types of glue, so it should not be left too long on a glued piece. Ammonia must be rinsed from the surface very well and adequate drying time allowed—usually two days. Bleach, especially, must *not* be used on ammonia-damp wood.

Pie Safe   See TIN.

Tin   Some old pieces—such as pie safes (cupboards), trunks, iceboxes, and dry sinks—have large metal parts that are usually tin. When found in the rough, these tin parts are invariably rusty even under several coats of paint or shellac. Unless the tin is rusted all the way through, such pieces can be beautifully refinished with just a little extra care. The wooden parts are, of course, stripped and subsequently refinished in the normal manner.

The tin should be cleaned as much as possible with regular stripper and a scrub brush to remove any old finish and some of the rust. Next, a rust remover is used. We prefer any one of several brands which come in a thick jellylike form as is available in hardware and paint stores. Rust Eater by the Turtle Wax Company is a good one. Naval Jelly is another brand but difficult to find in smaller localities.

These removers make relatively quick work of rust removal when used as directed on the container. This process is usually carried out with the tin in place, but it can be taken off the piece. Having tried a number of powdered rust removers, we have yet to discover one that gives satisfactory results.

Incidentally, tin should be protected from further rusting. This is done with a coat of clear spray plastic (which should not be allowed to get on the wood) or with a coat of varnish applied at the same time that it is applied to the wood. We consider it a sacrilege to paint over tin. One of the *potentially* most beautiful pie safes we have seen was ruined by some commercial refinisher who had painted the tin in a vain attempt to match the wood. To make matters worse, he reversed the tin in its frame—i.e., turned the rough side to the inside. But, then, the owners were quite happy. That's what makes the world go around!

Trunks   See TIN.

The Next Process

Your project piece has been through the stripping process. It is completely free of old finish and is in a condition very similar to what it was when first constructed. The differences are that it does have some stain; the surfaces are smoother; and the piece, if old or antique, shows signs of years of use. You are ready for the next process.

The ''Refinisher's Pathfinder,'' printed again on page 50, indicates that the choice of the next process depends on the final finish you wish to achieve. Following down the column headed by that finish type, the next number gives you the process and the location of the instructions. In each case, however, there are asterisks indicating that one or more intermediate processes may be necessary.

Bleaching (Chapter 6) is needed if the stripped piece is too dark for your purposes. The stain that remains after stripping may be bleached without changing the natural color of the wood. In addition, the wood itself may be bleached with another procedure. If, however, you do not wish to lighten the piece or any part of it, the bleaching chapter may be skipped.

Chapter 7, ''Basic Repairing,'' is the next optional chapter. It contains directions for making all types of repairs except relatively minor

REFINISHER'S PATHFINDER

SOFT Sealer-Wax	OIL	HARD Varnish Shellac Lacquer	PROCESSES	RE-FINISHER'S ENAMEL	MILK PAINT	ENAMEL AND FLAT PAINT
	CLEAR FINISHES "Natural Wood"				OPAQUE FINISHES Paint	
①	①	①	STRIPPING Chapter 5	⊛	⊛	⊛
⊛	⊛	⊛	BLEACHING Chapter 6			
⊛	⊛	⊛	BASIC REPAIRING Chapter 7	⊛	⊛	⊛
②	②	②	STAINING AND SEALING Chapter 8			
⊛	⊛	⊛	SURFACE REPAIRING Chapter 9	⊛	⊛	⊛
			PAINTING Chapter 10	①	①	①
	③	③	CLEAR FINISHING Chapter 11	②		⊛
③	④	④	DRESSING AND MAINTAINING Chapter 12	③	②	②

① Necessary sequential processes
⊛ Optional processes

defects in the surface. Basic repairs include such things as loose joints, missing parts, split boards, peeling veneer, and warps.

A necessary process for *all* pieces that are to be given a clear finish is staining and sealing. Whether or not any of the preceding optional processes have been used, the refinisher must use this process. Instructions are found in Chapter 8, "Staining and Sealing."

If the project piece is to be given a paint finish, Chapter 8 is omitted entirely. Repairs to the surface may be needed (Chapter 9). Painting instructions are found in Chapter 10.

6

Bleaching

Types of Bleaching

The process of bleaching a piece of furniture is actually two processes. Though many different chemicals may be used, each one does one of two separate and distinct jobs. One of these bleaching processes is frequently needed on old pieces. The other is needed very seldom and should never be used in place of the first.

It is quite common for old pieces, especially tables, chests, and the like, to be marred by stains of various types. Such stains are usually in the form of dark rings or circles caused by water that soaked down into the wood. Some dark stains were caused by a combination of heat and moisture. A few will be found that were caused by ink or other substances soaking into the wood.

While these stains are usually visible on the piece before refinishing is begun, they show up even more after the piece has been stripped. Of course, some will be hidden by the old finish and not even appear until it has been stripped.

Such marring stains should be removed before a new finish is applied. The stripping process will *not* remove them. They must be bleached out, and the time to do it is now—right after the stripping. This, the most common bleaching process, is discussed in detail in the following section. It is easy when done correctly. Once again we admonish you *not* to use sandpaper.

The same bleaching process is also used for another purpose. Occasionally, an old piece will have had a very dark and deep stain applied at some time in the past. After several applications of stripper, some of it is still down there deep in the wood. If the piece is to be refinished in its natural wood color, it will have to come out. Continued use of stripper will eventually remove it, but it is much easier and quicker to use bleach on the entire piece.

Until now we have discussed common bleaching. This process bleaches stains; it does *not* change the color of the wood itself. There may be times when you wish actually to lighten the color of the wood. Suppose (heaven forbid!) that a piece made of dark mahogany wood simply must be refinished to match one of the lighter woods. In this case, the color of the wood—not just the stain in the wood but the wood color—must be changed. Changing the natural color of wood requires the use of a wood bleach. Somewhat more often wood bleach may be used when stripping reveals that a piece has been constructed of more than one type of wood (see Chapter 3). It may be desirable to bleach the darker parts to more nearly match the lighter.

The materials and their proper use for bleaching stains are detailed in the following section. Bleaching wood is then discussed.

Bleaching Stains

Stains, whether of accidental or deliberate origin, are best removed with laundry bleach or oxalic acid. While either will do the job, we much prefer the use of laundry bleach, since it is easily obtained, requires no mixing, and is much less likely to raise the grain of the wood.

Clorox, or any brand of liquid laundry bleach that contains sodium hypochlorite as the active ingredient, may be used. It is applied in a well-ventilated room. SPECIAL CAUTION: *Never use bleach and ammonia together.* This combination of chemicals produces poisonous fumes. We do not even open the two bottles in the same room at the same time. You are urged to do the same.

To remove marring stains, usually in the form of black spots or rings, you must first bleach the entire surface. It is not necessary to bleach the entire piece—just the top or side containing the spot or spots. If you do not bleach the entire surface first, there will be a very light area where the dark spot was. The contrast between this area and the rest of the (unbleached) surface is too great to be easily hidden when the piece is stained later.

The procedure for bleaching is quite simple. Apply bleach straight from the bottle with a saturated cloth or sponge. The surface is kept moist for five or ten minutes. Then wipe the treated area several times with clean, water-soaked cloths. This is followed immediately by clean, dry cloths to remove all surface moisture.

At this point in the treatment you will not see much evidence that bleaching has taken place. This is caused by the wetness of the wood. When it dries it will be lighter. However, even while moist, you will still see the dark spot unless it was very light and shallow originally.

Now you must work on the stain itself. Apply more bleach to the stain and keep it moist for another five or ten minutes. This is the right time for a typical dark spot, but yours may require more time. The time is not critical—a few minutes too much will not matter. If you don't bleach the spot enough, you will find out when the surface dries, and the process may have to be repeated.

When you are bleaching the spot try to vary the position of the edges of the moist areas. This will prevent a sharp change in the color of the surface at any one place. Follow the bleach with wet and dry cloths as before.

Do not expect the spot to disappear while you are applying bleach. It will fade, but you will still be able to see it clearly. The spot will usually disappear within three or four hours as the wood dries. If it has not faded sufficiently in about four hours, bleach it further.

With some experience, you will learn to judge even sooner whether or not further bleaching is needed. Even the beginner need not wait until the wood is completely dry. The bleaching action is essentially complete after four hours.

Four hours, however, is not enough time for the wood to dry completely. You must allow at least twelve hours before starting another process. The actual time for thorough drying varies with temperature and humidity. Twenty-four hours will be ample in all but the most humid circumstances. With solid pieces, drying can be hastened by warm sunshine.

There are times when the refinisher wishes to lighten the color of a piece after it has been stripped. These pieces have had very dark stains which were applied by the manufacturer or an earlier refinisher. Sometimes the remaining stain is so dark that it obscures the grain of the wood.

You may remove such old applied stains by bleaching—the same process as stated above. Usually you will bleach all surfaces of a piece. The amount of bleaching required (time) depends, of course, on how much change of color is desired. You may go all the way back to the original wood color.

Another commonly used bleach for applied and accidental stains is *oxalic acid.* This dry chemical may be found in larger paint shops and drugstores. CAUTION: *Dry oxalic acid must not be inhaled. The use of a face mask is urged.*

About an ounce of oxalic acid is put in a cup of warm water. Stir this solution until no more of the crystals will dissolve. Undissolved oxalic acid is allowed to settle to the bottom, and the liquid is ready to use.

The oxalic-acid solution is applied with a brush. Keep the treated area moist for about twenty minutes and then allow it to dry. Remove the resulting dustlike particles with wet cloths. Again, a face mask is recommended to prevent inhalation of dry oxalic acid. This bleaching procedure may be repeated as necessary to remove the stains. Grade-O steel wool should be used to smooth the grain that is often raised by oxalic acid.

We do *not* recommend the use of oxalic acid. Laundry bleach works as well or better and has fewer disadvantages.

Bleaching Wood

The previously mentioned bleaches affect stains that have gotten into wood either accidentally or purposefully. They do not materially change the natural color of the wood itself. As a refinisher, this is the very effect you normally want—remove the added color but leave the natural wood color.

There may be a time, however, when you wish to lighten the color of the wood. Suppose that a pecan table is to be refinished in the shade of light oak. Or perhaps you find that a maple table has one walnut leg. Stripping the piece and bleaching the existing stain will not make the wood light enough. You must remove the wood color. Wood bleach is the product you must use.

We use Dexall's Wood Bleach. It works well, though there are other good brands on the market also. The chemicals used to bleach the color from wood are quite powerful, so you must take special care to follow carefully the instructions on your package. These bleaches consist of two separately packaged chemicals that must be used immediately on mixing. The mixture loses strength rapidly and will not keep. Care must be taken to avoid skin contact, to mix the chemicals only in a glass container, and to get the mixture only on the wood to be bleached. When used according to directions, wood bleach is quite safe.

Many stains are not affected by wood bleach. You may mix a small quantity and test it on the piece you have stripped. The chances are that you must first bleach the stain. In this case, bleach with Clorox as described earlier and *allow the wood to dry.* Then bleach the wood.

The procedure for using wood bleach is straightforward. Mix no more than a cupful at a time. Immediately apply it with a sponge, leaving a generous quantity on the wood to soak in. Mix more as needed to cover all surfaces. Then leave it alone to dry.

When the wood bleach has dried, you must sponge off the surface with water. This moisture will raise a slight fuzz on many woods, so the surface should be rubbed lightly with 4/0 steel wool when it has dried the second time.

You will not be able to see much difference in the color of the wood while it is moist. The beginner is likely to think that he has done something wrong. Wait until the wood dries thoroughly before reaching any conclusions. Then the surface will be much lighter; the wood will have lost a great deal of its original color. You may repeat the wood-bleaching process if the first application does not remove enough color for your purposes. A second application is seldom necessary.

The Next Process

When your piece is bleached to your satisfaction, the next refinishing process is "Basic Repairing" (Chapter 7). If you are applying a clear finish and no structural repairs are needed, you may skip to Chapter 8, "Staining and Sealing." If you are applying an opaque finish and the piece requires no basic repairs, you may turn to Chapter 9, "Surface Repairing," or Chapter 10, "Painting."

REFINISHER'S PATHFINDER

CLEAR FINISHES "Natural Wood"			PROCESSES	OPAQUE FINISHES Paint		
SOFT Sealer-Wax	OIL	HARD Varnish Shellac Lacquer		RE-FINISHER'S ENAMEL	MILK PAINT	ENAMEL AND FLAT PAINT
①	①	①	STRIPPING Chapter 5	✲	✲	✲
✲	✲	✲	BLEACHING Chapter 6			
✲	✲	✲	BASIC REPAIRING Chapter 7	✲	✲	✲
②	②	②	STAINING AND SEALING Chapter 8			
✲	✲	✲	SURFACE REPAIRING Chapter 9	✲	✲	✲
			PAINTING Chapter 10	①	①	①
	③	③	CLEAR FINISHING Chapter 11	②		✲
③	④	④	DRESSING AND MAINTAINING Chapter 12	③	②	②

① Necessary sequential processes
✲ Optional processes

7

Basic Repairing

Basic Repairs

At first thought it may appear that this chapter belongs in a book on woodworking. It is true that many of the same techniques are used in building and repairing furniture. The competent refinisher must be able to use some of these simple techniques. Old and antique pieces are rarely in new condition structurally. If a piece is worth refinishing, it is worth repairing. There is little point in having a refinished chair that is wobbly and rickety.

Because various types of repairs are made at different times during the refinishing processes, we have divided this discussion into two chapters. Surface or cosmetic repairs are made between staining and finishing a piece. Those instructions are given in Chapter 9. Basic or structural repairs are made between the stripping and staining processes. These are discussed in this chapter.

A good knowledge of basic repairing has a side benefit for the home refinisher. Not only is it necessary on many of the pieces he refinishes but it is valuable in purchasing furniture. Being able to judge the severity of defects in pieces in the marketplace is a decided advantage. We have seen potential purchasers pass up good buys on items that were much more easily repairable than they appeared. Conversely, high prices are often paid for items with complex defects that appear simple.

Before getting to specific instructions, the beginner should have a clear understanding of just what a repair is and what it is not. A valid and effective repair returns a piece as close as possible to its original condition. To accomplish this, the repairer does again what the builder did to the piece when he made it. A loose glue joint is reglued; it is not nailed, screwed, or corrugated. The legitimate repair makes use of *no* additional braces, mending plates, corner irons, or any such parts—wood or metal. If it was not there originally, it is not added. Of course, we are talking about good pieces. You may stabilize a junk table any way you can.

Gluing

The ability to join two parts with glue and do it well is of fundamental importance to the refinisher. Most repairs involve gluing or regluing parts together. This skill is so basic to repair work that we will consider it separately. Later we will discuss its application to various types of joints.

There are five rules for good gluing. They should be observed scrupulously if a joint is to be strong and lasting.

RULE 1: **A well-glued joint is greatly superior to one fastened by nails or screws.**

This is difficult for the beginner to believe. He has often seen glued joints that have been strengthened with nails or screws. Well, that is a case of seeing the cart before the horse. The fact is that these joints were fastened with screws or nails simply to hold them tightly while the glue dried. The glue does the holding. Later, the metal fasteners do no harm, and it was too much trouble to go back and remove them. When such joints become loose, they must be re-glued. The metal fasteners, even tightened, should not be depended on alone.

RULE 2: **The parts to be joined must be clean.**

Anything between the two surfaces other than fresh glue will weaken the joint. Dirt, old dried glue, and wax must be removed from both surfaces. Scrape the parts down to bare wood. Use any implement that will do the job—pocket knife, plane, X-acto blade, razor blade, or file. Get the surfaces clean, but remove as little wood as possible.

RULE 3: **The parts of a joint must be in good contact—that is, the surfaces must match.**

If two plane surfaces are to be joined, they must be straight and flat. Two *matching* irregular surfaces can be glued. An uneven surface does not glue well to a flat one. Surfaces that do not match should be shimmed—i.e., small wedges or splinters of wood should be used to fill the gaps. In a strong glued joint, wood is bonded to wood—not wood to glue to wood. In fitted joints (mortise and tenon corners, dowel and socket chair rungs, et cetera), any spaces must be filled with wood. After putting glue on the surfaces and fitting them together, all gaps are filled by driving in wooden splinters, match sticks, or toothpicks. Such "shims" are driven into the joint with a tack hammer and then cut off even with the surface.

RULE 4: **A glued joint must be made tight and immobile while drying.**

The joint that is shifted or allowed to shift before it is thoroughly dry will cause a problem. It may be weak; it may not hold at all; or it may dry in the wrong position. There are a number of methods for holding joints, and one or more will fit any situation.

As has been mentioned, nails or brads or screws can be used to hold parts together until the glue dries. Of course, such metal fasteners should not be used where they will interfere with the appearance or functioning of the parts. They may be removed when the joint is dry or they may be left in place.

In some cases, weights such as books or bricks may be put on the joint to compress and hold it. Kitchen-type waxed paper must be placed between the joint and the weight to keep them from being fastened together by glue squeezed out of the joint.

When gluing large or oddly shaped parts, a "tourniquet" can often be used to advantage. Chair legs and rungs, for example, can be held quite firmly with rope. A tourniquet is made by padding the parts to protect them, tying a soft rope around them, inserting a stick through the rope, and twisting the stick to tighten the rope. This may be done more conveniently (but no better) with a commercial "web clamp" that sells for a few dollars.

The most common method for holding a joint tight is to use clamps. The capacity of clamps varies from two inches to four feet and over. Even the home refinisher should have several clamps. Two or three clamps with at least a four-inch capacity will meet most needs. Those with wooden jaws are best, but they are quite expensive for occasional use. Metal C clamps are inexpensive and very satisfactory when used with a "clamp sandwich."

If clamps are put directly on furniture, they will, of course, mar the surface of the wood. For this reason it is necessary to use wooden blocks between the jaws of the clamp and the piece. The most

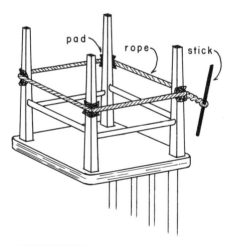

TOURNIQUET CLAMP

satisfactory way to do this is to use what we call a clamp sandwich. The piece is covered on both sides with waxed paper, and a piece of ¾-inch board is placed over each paper. The clamp is then tightened across the "sandwich" of scrap board, waxed paper, glued joint, waxed paper, and scrap board. Thus, the parts are not marred and the scrap boards don't become stuck by any excess glue that is forced out of the joint.

Large pieces stretched across table or chest tops may be held by the tourniquet method. More satisfactory are clamp ends that fit on any length of pipe. They may be purchased for just a few dollars and are quite as effective as cabinetmakers' clamps costing many times as much.

RULE 5: **Do not remove the clamps until the glue is thoroughly dry.**

This rule may seem insulting, but many a glued joint has been ruined by simple haste. Glues do not attain their full bonding power

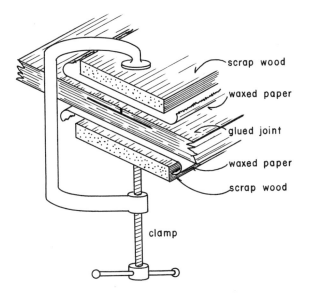

CLAMP SANDWICH

until they are *completely* dry. Many must be allowed additional time to "cure" or "set."

No fixed rule about the proper length of time can be given. Obviously, minimum time depends on the type of glue, but it also depends on the type of joint, the amount of glue used, and the temperature and humidity in the drying room. A very rough rule of thumb is to allow twenty-four hours for drying. The beginner should keep in mind that while he can release the clamp too soon, he can't leave it on too long. If there is any doubt, leave the joint clamped a little longer.

Those are the basic rules of gluing. Following them will result in good strong glue joints. Gluing is just that simple. Breaking these rules will surely cause problems. It is bad enough to have a drawer fall apart in use or perhaps not even fit into its case. It is most embarrassing to have a chair, the product of your handiwork, unceremoniously fall apart and dump a visitor to the floor!

There is one other matter that should be taken care of before the glue dries. Excess glue invariably runs out of a joint when it is clamped. Of course, a blob of dried glue is unsightly, but the refinisher has a greater concern. Glue that has dried on an exposed surface will interfere with proper staining and finishing. It must be removed completely. This is easier to do before the glue dries. If using the recommended glues, a damp cloth will wipe away wet glue. In many situations this is readily accomplished. The beginner may have some difficulty when using weights or a clamp sandwich to hold a joint. Our best advice is to use hand pressure to squeeze out as much glue as possible before clamping. The real secret is to use just enough but not too much glue, but that comes only with experience. Dried surface glue is removed with steel wool and ammonia.

Many kinds of glue are available. We have found three types to meet all our requirements. For most repairs we use the familiar white liquid glue that comes in plastic bottles. This glue is readily available in many kinds of stores, and there are a number of brands. Tite-Grip and Elmer's are two we use. They keep well, are easy to use, dry clear, and make good strong joints.

We use another type of glue where greater strength is needed. Weldwood or a similar powdered glue is mixed with water to a creamy consistency. It provides a stronger bond than white liquid glue and should be used for a joint that must stand up under a great deal of stress. A repair to the leg of a pedestal table, for example, requires this extra strength.

With both the liquid and the powdered glues, the joint should not be clamped too soon. A better bond will result if the glue has several minutes to soak into the wood before the excess is squeezed out.

The third type of glue will not be used often, but it is very convenient at times. This glue is called "contact cement"—Elmer's is one of the good brands. We use it for parts of awkward shape that defy clamping. It is also used for that occasional emergency when there is not time for our "regular" glue to dry.

Contact cement must be used with great care. Once the parts are touched together they cannot be shifted. Since they stay the way they are placed, the position of the parts must be right the first time.

Both sides of the joint are coated with a thin layer of contact cement. They are allowed to dry *apart*. Drying time is usually ten to fifteen minutes—check the label. When the cement is dry, the joint is touched together. That's it—no clamping and no waiting needed; no mistakes allowed. Obviously, contact cement cannot be used for joints that must be "slid" together like mortise and tenon, for example.

The right glue and the right procedures will produce good joints. Because so many repairs involve gluing, the beginning refinisher must acquire the simple skills required.

Repairing Loose Joints

The refinisher often encounters old joints in which the original glue has lost its hold. Repairing such loose joints is just a matter of following the rules for gluing given above. A few observations may help the beginner.

Whenever possible, the loose joint should be taken completely apart. In this manner each part may be cleaned of old glue more thoroughly. If the joint cannot be disassembled, the cleaning will take longer and probably not be as thorough. It is usually *not* advisable to attempt to take good joints apart in order to disassemble a bad one.

The home refinisher is advised to figure out his clamping method *before* applying glue. Sometimes clamping a joint becomes complicated, requiring the use of two or three clamps. This depends on the shapes of the parts and the location on the piece of the joint. On rare occasions it may be necessary to saw the scrap block to a special shape or even construct a simple jig to which to clamp the parts of the joint. Put the glue on only after you know how you will clamp it.

Care must be taken to be sure that a joint is held at the correct angle while drying. Fortunately, this is nearly always a right angle, and only a simple "try square" is needed to true it up.

Repairing Veneer

A good portion of every refinisher's repair work will be with veneer. The best quality veneer may separate, split, shrink, and even break after years of use. This is true especially if the piece has not been maintained properly. Certainly, accidents and abuse occur also.

Conditions often cause veneer to separate from its base. Unglued but otherwise undamaged veneer usually occurs at the edge of a surface, but it may be found as a "bubble" or "blister" in the middle. Some of the old glues were water-soluble—get them wet or even damp and the parts pop loose. Some were also sensitive to heat, and these are the easiest to repair.

Because it is so simple, heat repair should be tried first just in case it will work. The inside should be cleaned—not of glue this time, just of any dirt or wax that may be present. The loose veneer is covered with clean white paper (waxed paper if the veneer has a finish) and several layers of newspapers. A warm pressing iron is applied—*no* steam. The trick is to get enough heat to remelt the glue but not enough to harm the veneer. Lift the iron and the papers to check frequently. When the veneer appears to be trying to stay down, apply a little more heat. Then quickly remove the iron and put on a big stack of books to hold the veneer down until the glue cools. Should you get no sticking effect with the iron, give it up and reglue.

Regluing loose veneer is a matter of following the gluing rules. The effectiveness of the cleaning operation will depend on the size of the separation. With edge separations, glue can be applied more easily if the part is vertical. Using a blade and a piece of fine wire, push and lead the glue down into the separation as far as possible. Really get it down there; just gluing the outside edge is *not* sufficient. After most of the excess glue has been squeezed out by hand pressure, the repair is weighted or clamped.

Veneer blisters or bubbles are a little more difficult to glue down. Two approaches are available. The first, more suitable with larger areas, involves cutting right down the grain through the middle of the blister. A *new* razor blade is used so that the edges will be smooth-cut. One half and then the other half of the blister top is gently pried up so that glue can be inserted.

The second approach to repairing a veneer blister requires the use of a glue injector. This little instrument is inexpensive but may be difficult to find locally. It functions in the manner of a hypodermic. To use the glue injector, a very small hole is drilled carefully in the top of the blister. Glue is injected into the blister and weights or clamps used. The hole itself probably will have to be repaired later. It is handled like a tack hole. This type of surface or cosmetic repair is treated in Chapter 9.

If the veneer damage includes splits or breaks, the pieces must be fitted together as carefully as possible and reglued in the usual manner. When dry, any ridges must be shaved down with a razor blade. Any small crevices are given a surface-repair treatment later.

Cases involving broken and missing pieces of veneer are much more difficult to repair. Perfect results are all but impossible to achieve without replacing the veneer on the entire surface. Acceptable repairs can be made with patience and fortitude. The best procedure is to cut the edges of the remaining veneer into straight lines. A metal straight-edge and a new, perfect razor must be used. The resulting "hole" need not be square or rectangular, but the edges must be absolutely clean-cut.

The next task in this repair is to find a piece of veneer that is larger than the hole, has a matching type of grain, and is of the proper thickness. Sometimes it can be removed from an unexposed part of the same piece of furniture or from a junk piece. It may be necessary to purchase new veneer.

Whatever its source, the new section must be trimmed carefully with straight-edge and new razor blade to fit into the hole. Reasonably small crevices may be given a surface repair after the piece is stained.

Extensively damaged veneer that is beyond repair must be removed entirely. If a suitable sheet of new veneer can be located, it may be glued to the base. The base surface itself may be cleaned, stained, and finished. Assuming this is the top of a table or chest, a third alternative is to cover the base with a piece of marble. None of these leaves the refinisher with an authentic antique, but the resulting piece may be handsome as well as useful.

There are two reasons for removing veneer. It must be removed if it is to be replaced. Sometimes veneer can be repaired more easily if it is first removed. You may even run into cases in which the veneer has shrunk and pulled up so badly that your only recourse is to take it up and reglue it altogether.

Removing veneer is not as bad a job as it may appear. You recall that we stated earlier that nearly all veneer glues are affected by water or heat or both. We will use this fact in the removal process. Since water is easier to handle, we always try it first and hope that it does the job.

Now it is possible to leave the piece out in the rain or soak it in a tub for a week or so. Water-soluble glue would dissolve and the veneer would pop off. While easier, this method is likely to cause irreparable damage to the wood itself. It is much better to control the amount of water soaking into the wood.

We use a small plastic "squirt bottle" filled with *warm* water and a long, dull knife blade. The blade is used to lift the veneer gently so that the water can be squirted or dripped directly on the edge of the still holding glue. Water-soluble glue will gradually release a little at a time. Care must be taken to get the veneer up evenly or the wood may be strained to the splitting or breaking point.

If no progress is made within about ten minutes, you may assume that the glue is not soluble in water. In this case, you must use the heat method. This is done with a pressing iron in the manner described earlier except that the purpose is to separate rather than reglue. Beginning at an edge, the blade is used to separate the veneer as the heat softens the glue. Often it is helpful to slip a piece of waxed paper into the separation as it enlarges in order to keep it from becoming reattached. In this heat process, the newspaper may be eliminated if you are removing worthless veneer.

When the veneer has been entirely removed, it is necessary to clean all the remaining glue from the surface. Ammonia straight from the bottle may be used for this purpose. Coat the surface well and, after about five minutes, rinse with wet cloths. Repeat as necessary to clean the surface completely. Allow sufficient drying time before the next process (regluing or staining).

Pieces of removed veneer that are not reused should be stored away for use in future repairs. Veneer that is warped can be straightened as described earlier for thicker pieces.

Repairing Splits, Cracks, Breaks

We shall make no distinction between a split in an individual board and one between two boards that had been glued together to form a surface. Both are handled the same way. Two pieces of wood have separated and must be put back together with glue.

The repair is quite simple if the parts have separated completely and have not splintered. The edges are cleaned; glue is applied; and the parts are clamped. The clamping can be touchy, as the parts must be aligned at the ends and along the joined edges on the side that will be exposed. Further, the two parts must be flat or straight from side to side. This can be done with a tourniquet, but the task is much simpler with pipe or cabinetmakers' clamps.

Repairs to an old joint that has separated for only a part of its length or a split that extends only part way down a board require more patience. Some refinishers will advise that the parts be separated completely. We do not take that approach, since it may cause splintering, and that is real trouble.

We use any and every kind of blade to clean out the split as much as possible without lengthening it. The board is then placed on end and glue is fed into the vertical separation. Gravity, blades, wire, and flexing the parts are all used to get the glue down where it seemed impossible at first. Then the parts are clamped and allowed to dry.

A splintered board is another matter. If the splintering is not extensive, it may be possible to fit the several parts together even if it must be done in stages. If the upper (exposed) surfaces are in reasonably good shape, the parts may be assembled with hidden dowels across the split—a painstaking procedure. A board that is splintered extensively and one that is broken *across* the grain will have to be replaced or the piece discarded.

Repairing Drawers

Drawers from old pieces frequently require several repairs. They suffer from several common ailments. One of these, loose joints, was discussed earlier.

Often well-used drawers will not slide properly in their cases. This can be caused by one or more of several defects. First to be checked are the guides. These are small strips of wood in the case which keep the drawer motion straight in and out. The guides may be worn, loose, broken, or missing entirely. If present, they may be repairable, but it is usually more satisfactory to replace them.

Excessive wear can prevent proper operation of drawers. The refinisher should examine the bottom edges of the drawer sides and the upper edge of the runner on which they slide. One or both parts may be worn so much that the bottom of the drawer drags or hangs on the runner. Grooves worn in the runner may be repaired with small, shaped wooden blocks or they may be filled with wood filler that is available in paste or powder form.

Worn bottom edges of drawer sides may be built up with wood filler. A more satisfactory repair is to add wood strips. The bottom edges do not wear the same amount along their length, so they must be straightened. This can be done with a small snub-nose plane or a carefully wielded chisel. When the edge is straight, a strip of the

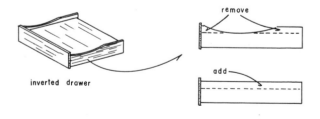

inverted drawer

REPAIRING WORN DRAWER

proper width and height is glued on to replace the missing wood. A little paraffin rubbed on the runner and the sides *after the finish has been applied* will make any drawer slide better.

The bottom board of an old drawer is another common problem. Wood shrinks when it dries out, and the bottom board often appears to have been cut off short. Usually all that is necessary is to remove the brads that hold the board to the back of the drawer and slide it forward, replacing the brads to hold it there. Sometimes the shrinkage is so great that this leaves a gap at the rear. Such a gap must be filled with a board of the proper dimensions.

Correcting Warps

As was mentioned in the preceding section, wood shrinks as it dries out. For all practical purposes we can consider that this shrinkage takes place entirely *across* the grain. Thus, a board will become narrower but not shorter.

All too often old pieces were finished only on the exposed surfaces. The inner surfaces were left unfinished and raw. Such a board can lose little or none of its moisture content through the finish. The raw side, however, can and does lose moisture in heated and dry houses over the years. The raw side shrank more than the finished side, became narrower, and the board bent or warped in that direction.

Knowing what caused a board to warp, the refinisher knows how to straighten it. Incidentally, it also gives him the best possible reason for refinishing a piece *completely*—i.e., both inside and out. Cor-

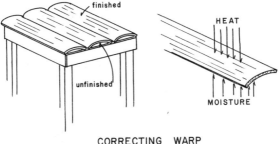

CORRECTING WARP

recting a warp is a matter of balancing the uneven moisture content of the wood.

First, the board must be completely stripped of old finish. Of course, this was done when the entire piece was stripped. It is also necessary to remove the board from the piece in order to work on it. The idea is to add moisture to the dry (concave) side and take it out of the "wet" (convex) side.

The board is placed so that the wet side is heated, taking care not to scorch it. This may be done by placing it over a radiator or heat vent in the winter, over heat lamps (careful), or in hot summer sunshine. While the convex side is being heated (and dried), the dry side is kept moist with damp cloths. This is a slow process. It may be hastened a little by applying a *limited* amount of pressure in the right direction with weights or clamps. Obviously, too much pressure will cause the board to crack and so loss of the game.

When the board is straight or even warped a little in the opposite direction, it is stood on end in the finishing room and allowed to dry for a few days. Usually, the result is a fairly even board, but if too much of the original warp returns, the process must be repeated.

Replacing Parts

The beginning refinisher may be tempted to replace damaged parts. After all, it is often *easier* to make and install a new part than to repair an old one. This impulse must be resisted. It is axiomatic among professional refinishers that *no* repairable part is replaced.

Certainly, a missing part may have to be replaced in order to make a piece usable. A part that is damaged beyond repair may be replaced. The point is that a piece with a replacement part is no longer "original" or "authentic." Its value is diminished by the new part.

If a part must be replaced, it is preferable to use old wood rather than new. There are several possible sources of old wood. Doors, door and window framing, stair rails, wainscoting, and similar items may be secured from an old house being torn down. They can be found in some salvage yards. Odd table leaves can be purchased in many "antique shops." Old furniture that is beyond repair may have some good parts. If new wood must be used, it must be well seasoned.

The replacement part should be cut out carefully, doing any necessary matching of shape. In this case, it is legitimate and even necessary to use sandpaper and/or a power sander—this is construction, not refinishing! When the part fits well, it should be fastened down in a manner appropriate to the piece. Frequently, a replacement part will not stain like the original parts. Techniques for achieving matching tones are discussed in the following chapter.

Miscellaneous Repairs

If you, the home refinisher, continue in this work, you will encounter a wide variety of repair problems. Most can be solved with a little thought and ingenuity. We will mention three others here.

Burns   In spite of the Surgeon General, cigarette burns on furniture will always be with us. You can handle the very minor ones with abrasion. Steel wool around a fingertip will remove the discolored wood. Deeper ones may have to be scraped lightly with a curved blade. *All* the discoloration need not be removed, as the stain will help to conceal some of it. Minor depressions need not be filled, as the body of the finish and dressing will tend to fill them. Of course, deep burns will have to be dug into. These must receive surface repairs per Chapter 9.

Dents   Surface dents are quite easy to remove if they are not so severe that the fibers of the wood have been broken. Apply a steam pressing iron to the problem. Hold the iron above the surface (do not touch) and aim the steam at the dent. Often the dent will rise to its original level. If not, broken fibers are preventing expansion, and it must be filled (Chapter 9).

Legs   A short or a long leg on a piece can be a very annoying problem when treated incorrectly. We once had a six-legged table in the shop that gave us quite a run before it was stabilized. Some pieces are so constructed that the legs can be removed with little trouble. This is the easiest kind to repair. Remove the short leg or legs and put a shim—a thin piece of wood—on top of it. This shim between the leg and the bottom of the top will effectively lengthen the leg. Sometimes, however, the only solution is to make the long leg or legs shorter.

Surely you have seen the cartoon character who was trying to even a table by cutting the longest leg. Each time he cut a little too much and had to cut some off another leg to make up for his mistake. He finally ended up with six-inch legs on his kitchen table! The cartoon is quite amusing but *it can happen to you.*

First and foremost, don't cut or saw a leg to make it shorter. The differences in length are very small. Use a file or a wood rasp, which is nothing but a rough file. Take off only a little wood at a time—no power tools here. Check frequently on a surface that you *know* to be flat. We usually put the piece up on the workbench and slide the long leg off the edge to file it. Then it is only necessary to slide it back on the bench to check the length.

Holes, Crevices, Gouges, Cracks   Damage of this type is not repaired at this phase of the refinishing processes. They are repaired *after* the piece has been stained. Instructions are provided in Chapter 9: "Surface Repairing."

Hardware

All that was said about replacing wood parts applies as well to hardware. If at all possible, original hardware should be retained. This applies not only to hinges, drawer pulls, escutcheons, and brass tips but to nails, brads, and screws as well. Repair of such parts as hinges may require some concealed welding or brazing, but you should have this done.

The home refinisher should be alert to spot second- and third-generation hardware. Drawer pulls, especially, will have often been replaced. You can spot replacements by marks in the wood made by the original hardware. Often the style of newer pulls is not appropriate to the piece.

Previously replaced hardware nearly always should be replaced. The exception is when the replacements themselves are of such an age that they have value. Good-quality reproduction drawer pulls may be ordered or purchased in most large cities. You may be fortunate enough to find a set on a junk piece. Be sure that you choose an appropriate style—Queen Anne pulls are quite out of place on a Victorian chest.

Hinges can be particularly troublesome. This is especially true of those on drop-leaf tables. When we find a drop-leaf that does not

REFINISHER'S PATHFINDER

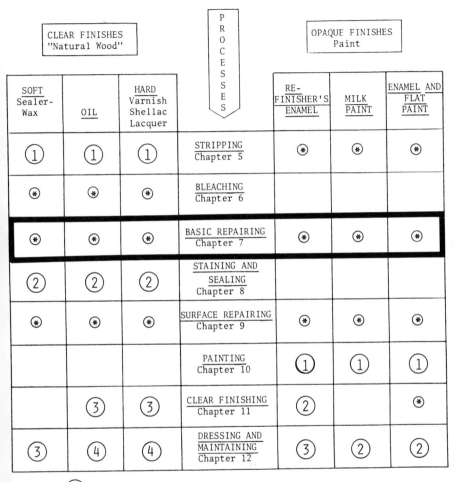

CLEAR FINISHES "Natural Wood"			PROCESSES	OPAQUE FINISHES Paint		
SOFT Sealer-Wax	OIL	HARD Varnish Shellac Lacquer		RE-FINISHER'S ENAMEL	MILK PAINT	ENAMEL AND FLAT PAINT
①	①	①	STRIPPING Chapter 5	⊛	⊛	⊛
⊛	⊛	⊛	BLEACHING Chapter 6			
⊛	⊛	⊛	BASIC REPAIRING Chapter 7	⊛	⊛	⊛
②	②	②	STAINING AND SEALING Chapter 8			
⊛	⊛	⊛	SURFACE REPAIRING Chapter 9	⊛	⊛	⊛
			PAINTING Chapter 10	①	①	①
	③	③	CLEAR FINISHING Chapter 11	②		⊛
③	④	④	DRESSING AND MAINTAINING Chapter 12	③	②	②

① Necessary sequential processes
⊛ Optional processes

function properly, it is due to a hinge in the wrong position or one of the wrong size. Hinge replacements must be exact in size and position.

The refinisher must exercise care in fastening and refastening hinges with screws. In this and all other cases, replacement screws must not be so large as to split old wood nor so long as to go clear through. It is a sad sight to see the point of a too long screw as it pushes up through the top of a table!

In old and antique pieces, screw holes will often be so enlarged that the original screw won't hold. Rather than using a larger screw, fill the hole with steel wool or a small piece of soft pine wood. This will enable the original screw to hold securely. In very severe cases it may be necessary to "plug" the old hole. Carefully drill out the hole several sizes larger than the original (don't drill all the way through). Fill the new hole by gluing in a dowel of the proper diameter and length. When the glue has dried, the screw will hold securely in a new hole in the dowel.

The Next Process

Your project piece stands before you now stripped of old finish, bleached as necessary, and structurally repaired. It is clean and sturdy. The next process depends on the type of finish you intend to apply.

If the piece will have an opaque finish, proceed to Chapter 9 for instructions for making surface or cosmetic repairs. Should none be needed, skip to Chapter 10: "Painting."

If the piece is to be given a clear finish, it must be stained and sealed. These instructions are in the next chapter (8).

8

Staining and Sealing

All wood that is to receive a clear finish should be stained and sealed. Sealing offers protection to the wood and improves the finish appearance. Staining can change or darken the color of the wood, but, more importantly, it brings out the grain and beauty. Staining is all but essential to get the best appearance even though the color is to be unchanged.

Types of Stains and Sealers

Stains and sealers are available in a variety of types. We do *not* recommend the use of separate stain and sealer. They require two different application operations and, thus, greater time and effort than the recommended combination. We use "sealer-stain," which does both jobs at once.

If you wish to use stain and sealer separately in a two-step operation, you can achieve equally good results. Penetrating stain is applied in the same manner as sealer-stain, described below. If you use "oil penetrating" or "penetrating" or any nonsealing stain, be sure to use sealer also. Sealer is applied with a brush, allowed to soak in, and the excess wiped away with a cloth.

We prefer to get on with the refinishing and seal and stain in one operation. The results are the same. The product is labeled *sealer-stain* or *sealing-stain,* and there are a number of brands. We have found that those manufactured by Minwax ("wood finish") yield consistently good results. (The beginner should know that Minwax is not the name of a wax. It is the name of a company that produces a good line of refinishing products.) The Acme SPEE-D-DRY brand sealer-stains are also quite reliable. Both brands produce good results with minimum effort, mix well, and keep well when the can is closed carefully.

Though the instructions that follow are generally applicable to nonsealing stains, they refer specifically to the use of sealer-stains. For convenience we shall use the word *stain* to mean a product that both stains and seals.

The beginner is cautioned not to confuse any of the foregoing with "varnish-stain." This is a completely different type of product for a different use. It is difficult to get acceptable results with varnish-stain. We neither use nor recommend varnish-stain for any purpose.

Choosing the Color

Stains are available in an often bewildering variety of colors, tones, and shades. The refinisher is faced with the task of selecting one that will produce the desired results. This is more complex than it may appear.

You will want your stain to do one of three things: bring out the grain with little or no change in coloring; bring out the grain and darken the color; or bring out the grain and change the color to that of another wood. Obviously, the color is the thing.

Any substance applied to wood will change its appearance slightly. Since sealer-stain, finish, and dressing must be applied, refinished wood does not look exactly like it did when raw. For those pieces which are to be changed in coloring as little as possible, there are several approaches. You may use a stain that matches the wood—oak on oak, cherry on cherry, walnut on walnut, and so on. In this case, choose the lightest shade available, light walnut, for example.

You may put light oak stain on any kind of wood. It has little pigment and causes little or no color change. Minwax produces a "natural" stain that has much the same result. It does intensify the grain but often not as much as a stain colored for the specific wood.

To darken the color, simply purchase a darker shade of stain—dark oak on oak and dark mahogany on mahogany, for example. A stain that is too light or too dark can be changed by following the mixing instructions given below.

Often a wood can be made to simulate another wood by the use of an appropriate stain. Walnut stain on a cherry table may produce a very satisfactory "walnut" table. Results are not as predictable in this type of staining. The refinisher must be careful of evident grain patterns as well as color. A "walnut" table with an oak grain would look strange indeed.

The problem in staining is not applying it but in predicting its final appearance. The fact is that it cannot be predicted accurately. Woods vary greatly in the way they take stains. A given stain on two kinds of wood will produce two different results. Not only that but a stain may produce different results on two pieces of the same kind of wood.

The only way to actually determine the effect of a given stain on a piece of furniture is to apply it and find out. The color charts at the store will give a reasonable approximation for most cases. Even better are the actual samples that some dealers have available. These samples are small pieces of various woods that have been stained with a selection of colors and shades. In this case you can see what light walnut stain looks like on birch wood.

Fortunately, *exact* colors are seldom necessary. Even so, we recommend that the selected stain be applied to a small trial spot on the back of the piece or on the inside of a drawer front. This trial will let you know what the final appearance will be.

Mixing and Matching Colors

The refinisher has frequent need to change the effect of a stain. He may wish to make it darker or lighter, more red or more brown, or any number and combination of changes. This is done by mixing.

The easiest and most often needed change is to make a stain darker. You may do this in either of two ways: by mixing in some color only or by mixing in a darker stain. Colors are available in several different bases, and you must be sure to use the right type with your brand of stain. Check the label, the manufacturer's literature, or the salesman's recommendation to determine what base you need.

Burnt umber is a good general darkening color. Put a little from the tube, can, or package into the can of stain. Use a small quantity —it goes a long way. Stir or shake the stain *thoroughly.* Failure to mix the color and the stain completely will result in an uneven, blotchy application. If the color is not dark enough, repeat the process with more color.

It is much more convenient to darken a stain by mixing in some darker stain. Pour some into the lighter stain and stir them together (much less stirring than that required when mixing a color). In order to avoid the mistake of mixing base types, mix together stains of the same brand.

If a stain is to be lightened or otherwise changed (redder, browner, blacker), this may be done with colors or with other stains. The home refinisher will find colors harder to handle, and he is not likely to have a selection in his shop. In some cases a combination of colors is needed to achieve the desired result. We recommend that you mix stains together.

A stain is lightened by adding some "natural" or light oak stain. Tints are changed by mixing in an appropriate stain—mahogany, walnut, cherry, jacobean.

You will find it a good practice to change the label on any can of mixed stain. The new label should describe the new color or give the mixture used (light oak and walnut). It is more helpful to state the approximate proportions used (ten light oak and one dark walnut). Such labeling can save you trouble when you use a half-filled can from the shelf. It can also help you mix the same color stain later.

As mentioned earlier, it is not often necessary to match stains exactly. In the typical home setting, two pieces of furniture as little as two feet apart can be quite different, yet appear the same. Occasionally, however, two parts on one piece do need to be matched quite closely.

When you run across one of those old pieces made from two or more kinds of wood, you may wish to disguise this if the grains are not too dissimilar. To do so, the use of different stains on the different woods is usually necessary. The same situation may arise in the case of a replacement part.

The only way to match such staining is by trial and error. Mix something that looks right and try it. Change it slightly and try again. The beginner may have to try a number of times before getting a satisfactory match. Experience will decrease the number of trials necessary.

Sometimes there is no inconspicuous place on each part to try stains for matching. In such circumstances, you will have to use the areas that are available. When the match is satisfactory, the trial areas must be stripped again before the final stains are applied.

Applying Stain

The basic idea in staining is to put it on the wood, let it soak in, and wipe off the excess. The process is just that simple and it may be done in several ways. Our recommended method follows.

Stain may be applied with a brush or a cloth. We prefer to use a cloth for greater control of quantity and evenness of application. In this case a small brush must be used to get stain all the way into corners, crevices, and deep carvings. Otherwise, cloth and brush application is the same.

The cloth (or brush) should be well loaded with stain but not dripping. Stain is not applied to the entire piece at once. One surface or part is completed before proceeding to the next.

The stain is brushed or rubbed on a surface quickly in a helter-skelter manner. Then it is roughly evened out by rubbing lightly in one direction. When the stain has had enough time to soak in sufficiently, the surface is wiped with a clean dry cloth.

The timing of the wiping operation is important but not critical in most cases. The more time between applying and wiping, the more the stain soaks in and the darker the surface will be. We cannot even give you a rule-of-thumb. The timing may be anything between a minute or two and thirty minutes. The time in any given case is determined by the wood, the color and type of stain, and the desired color of the piece. The refinisher should allow about the same amount of time that he allowed on his trial spot.

The wiping action should be firm and in one direction (usually with the grain). As soon as the surface is wiped, stain is applied to the next surface and the procedure repeated.

Throughout this process the stain should be stirred from time to time. This prevents the pigment from settling to the bottom and causing the stain to be lighter on the last surface than on the first. We keep a small stick or paddle in the open can and give it an occasional twirl.

Every surface that you can reach should be stained. This includes the bottom surface of table and chest tops, the inner surfaces of sides and skirts, inner and outer backs, and the inside and outside of all drawer parts. The well-refinished piece is stained and finished all over. The reason is not so much the appearance but protection of the wood, as is discussed in a subsequent chapter.

You should apply stain in a well-ventilated and clean room. Ideally, the temperature should be around 70 degrees and the humidity low, though a wide range is permissible in both of these factors with most materials. Begin with the piece standing on clean newspapers. Of course, you will work from the highest to the lowest surfaces to keep drips from falling on completed areas. With many pieces, especially tables, you will find it more convenient to start with the piece upside down. When the undersides are stained, you can place the piece upright and stain the upper surfaces.

When staining is completed, allow the piece to dry twelve to twenty-four hours, depending on the humidity. Follow this with 3/0 steel wool rubbed in the direction of the grain. The steel wool smooths irregularities, removes settled dust, and assists in evening the stain coat. Exercise care on corners and edges to keep the steel wool from biting down into the wood.

Pieces or parts of pieces that are to receive a second application of stain must be cleaned thoroughly of steel particles. Second (and third) applications of stain usually do not soak in as quickly as did the first.

End Grain

The exposed end grain of a board occasionally creates problems in staining. The edges running parallel with the grain take stain just as do the top and bottom. Where the board has been cut across the grain, however, it has a tendency to soak up stain thirstily. This is particularly true in the cases of softer woods and of rougher edges. As a result, such end grain often stains much darker than other surfaces.

The beginning refinisher should understand that darker end grain is not always undesirable. In fact, it frequently adds a warmth and beauty to a piece. We believe that it becomes objectionable when there is a severe contrast in color. Simply applying less stain to the end grain is seldom satisfactory. Excessive contrast can be avoided in several ways.

You can wipe stain from the end grain before wiping it from the other surfaces. This gives the stain less time to soak in and results in a lighter edge. This technique is most effective with the hardest woods but will provide no relief when used with woods of middle hardness.

A second method for avoiding dark end grains is to use a lighter stain. Separate a small quantity of the stain to be used on the piece and lighten it by mixing as explained earlier. The softer the wood, the lighter the end grain stain should be made. With a mixture of the correct shade, this technique is quite effective. Its use does require careful work at the corners where end grain and other surfaces meet.

Of course, you can wipe the end grain with a cloth moistened with paint thinner. If this is done immediately after the excess stain is wiped away, the end grain will be several shades lighter. You will have more difficulty avoiding damage to adjoining stained surfaces with this method.

The last technique we shall mention is more difficult to control and is more time-consuming. A very thin shellac is used—about one part shellac to two parts denatured alcohol. Apply this to the end grain, taking great care that none gets on adjoining surfaces. After several hours when the shellac is dry, the pores of the end grain will be partially closed and it will not soak up stain so readily. We do not recommend this method to the beginner because of the skill required —too much shellac and the stain will not soak in at all; too little shellac and the problem still exists.

Bleached Wood

When you have bleached a part of a piece, you must use some care in staining it. The bleached portion is lighter, of course, and usually will be lighter after staining. You may mix a quantity of darker stain for the bleached surface. We prefer to stain the piece normally, giving the lighter surface a second application of the original stain.

New Wood

The refinisher is faced occasionally with staining a piece that contains some new wood. It may be a replacement part for one damaged beyond repair or for one that was missing entirely. Even if the new part was made from old wood as recommended, it will have some new surfaces. Wood that has not been finished and stripped will not stain like wood that has been.

New wood and new surfaces stain more readily than stripped surfaces. The pores are more open and the stain is soaked up faster. If the new and old parts of a piece are to balance, allowances must be made.

Usually this problem can be avoided if you wipe stain off the new parts more quickly than from the old. Occasionally you may find it necessary to follow this with a cloth moistened with paint thinner. This will further lighten the new wood.

While the subject of unfinished furniture is not actually a refinishing topic, it should be mentioned here as "new wood." The home craftsman will be called on to stain such pieces sooner or later. Whether they are newly constructed or are commercially purchased, unfinished furniture is stained (and finished) in the same manner as is a stripped piece. One further point about such commercially available pieces: "Unfinished" means not only that a finish must be

REFINISHER'S PATHFINDER

CLEAR FINISHES "Natural Wood"			PROCESSES	OPAQUE FINISHES Paint		
SOFT Sealer-Wax	OIL	HARD Varnish Shellac Lacquer		RE-FINISHER'S ENAMEL	MILK PAINT	ENAMEL AND FLAT PAINT
①	①	①	STRIPPING Chapter 5	✳	✳	✳
✳	✳	✳	BLEACHING Chapter 6			
✳	✳	✳	BASIC REPAIRING Chapter 7	✳	✳	✳
②	②	②	STAINING AND SEALING Chapter 8			
✳	✳	✳	SURFACE REPAIRING Chapter 9	✳	✳	✳
			PAINTING Chapter 10	①	①	①
	③	③	CLEAR FINISHING Chapter 11	②		✳
③	④	④	DRESSING AND MAINTAINING Chapter 12	③	②	②

① Necessary sequential processes
✳ Optional processes

applied but also that the construction is unfinished. The purchaser must complete the last phase of construction. He must sand the piece thoroughly, removing all fuzz and every rough spot. *Then* he may proceed with the staining.

The Next Process

Your project piece stands before you stained, sealed, steel-wooled, and cleaned to your satisfaction. By this time you should know every inch of every surface intimately. You are aware of one or more surface blemishes that must be repaired. Those instructions will be found in the following chapter.

If you are fortunate enough to have a piece that needs no surface repairs, you are ready to apply the finish. Instructions for *soft* finishing are in Chapter 12. *Oil* and *hard* finishes are discussed in Chapter 11.

9

Surface Repairing

Surface Repairs

Damage to the exposed surface of a piece of furniture must be repaired with considerable care. Perhaps a rough and discolored patch does look better than the nail hole it fills, but an invisible one is even better. An "invisible" patch is almost impossible to achieve, but even the beginner can make repairs that do not call attention to themselves.

Anyone who works with furniture must be prepared to make good surface repairs. Burns, cracks, dents, gouges, and nail holes are found frequently in old furniture. Accidents do happen. Damage usually should be repaired whether the piece is old or new.

We will give you instructions for making surface repairs, but we cannot tell you whether or not you *should* do so. Most instances of surface damage will call obviously for repair. Frequently, however, it is not advisable to correct all minor defects. Some signs of age and use are desirable in many old pieces. Don't make repairs just because you know how! New furniture is expected to be perfect; reproductions are expected to be perfect; antiques are not. A perfect antique looks like a good reproduction.

The refinisher should not *over*repair surface defects. Certainly not to the extent done by one of our clients. Several years ago a gentleman sought advice about finishing a mahogany piece on which he was working. We examined the piece and were amazed to discover that he had meticulously "repaired" every hole in the wormy mahogany!

We shall give directions for repairing a "hole" such as may have been caused by a tack, a nail, or a screw. These directions apply equally well to cuts, cracks, dents, gouges—in fact, to any kind of depression in the surface. All these defects are handled alike, since the only significant difference among them is their shape.

Surface repairs may be divided into two types. We shall discuss them separately. The first includes those repairs to surfaces that are to receive an opaque (paint) finish. The second type of surface repair is that which is to be covered by a clear finish.

Surface Repairs Under Opaque Finishes

Repairs to surfaces that are to be painted are quite easy to make. The repair need be only even and smooth. The color of the filler is immaterial since it will not be visible through the paint. Because it will be covered by an opaque finish, a wide variety of substances may be used.

Commercial wood fillers are available in paste or dry form. The pastes are ready to use. The dry fillers must be mixed with water to a pastelike consistency. We generally use one of the premixed brands simply for convenience. While we have no special preference, Plastic Wood is a popular and reliable brand. Don't be concerned about the color since it won't show through the paint.

For occasional use, the home refinisher may find the dry filler more economical. Only the needed quantity is mixed for use. In the dry form it keeps indefinitely. The premixed fillers have a tendency to dry out in a partially filled can over a period of time. Either will make a good repair. In an emergency we have filled small holes with a mixture of glue and sawdust.

Small holes present no problem. They are packed with filler and smoothed with a clean, shiny blade. Excess filler should be wiped from the surrounding surface.

Sufficient drying time must be allowed. This is usually several hours, but check the label on your brand. A rough drying guide can be provided by a small quantity of filler placed on a scrap board. The guide filler does usually dry faster, so allow more time for your repair.

More extensive repairs must be handled somewhat differently. Larger quantities of wood filler dry out very slowly. It could be days before the filler in a large hole dries throughout. Couple this with the fact that many such fillers shrink a bit as they dry. The result is a repair that has shrunk to a level below the surrounding surface by the time it finally dries. The solution is to fill large holes in stages.

The bottom of the hole is packed with a small quantity of filler. The amount should be about the size of a typical pencil eraser. When this has dried, another quantity of filler is put into the hole and allowed to dry. This process is continued until the repair is complete.

Refinishers usually compensate for shrinkage of the filler when smoothing the final "layer" in a large repair. They make the surface of the filler slightly convex. When done just right, the shrinkage brings the surface down so that it is just even with the wood. You need not be so exact. Use too much filler rather than too little. If the surface protrudes slightly when dry, it can be made even by careful shaving with a razor.

When the filler is dry, even, and smooth, nothing more need be done. The piece is ready for painting (Chapter 10).

Surface Repairs Under Clear Finishes

Surface defects on a piece that is to receive one of the clear finishes present an added complexity to the refinisher. The repair itself can be *seen*. Obviously, the filler substance must match the piece in color. This is easier to say than to do.

It would be nice if there were a substance that could be used to fill the hole *before* staining the piece. Then the repair and the wood could be stained at the same time and be the same color and be practically invisible. Yes, that would be nice, but it doesn't work out that way.

Over the years we have tried everything that we could find. We have found no fillers that take stain just the way wood takes it. Further, it stands to reason that no one filler could take stain like pine when it is in pine and like oak when it is in oak. A repair made before staining with any filler known to us will stand out like a sore thumb after staining. That is the reason why this chapter follows the staining process chapter. Stain first; repair second.

For the sake of completeness, the exception to these statements should be mentioned. Certainly, wood stains like wood! A repair made with a "patch" or "plug" of closely matched wood can be done before staining and later be invisible. Such a repair requires hours of effort by a highly skilled craftsman. It is *not* for the home refinisher. Very few professional refinishers can do this job well. If they try it, most end up repairing the repair, so they do it another way. They use color-matched fillers *after* the piece is stained. You can do the same thing.

Most surface repairs under clear finishes are made with nothing more complex than wax. When a hole is filled with wax of the proper color, it blends into the surrounding surface and is all but invisible. The process requires patience and a degree of skill. With a little practice, however, even an amateur can make a repair, turn away for a moment, and have to search to locate it again.

Perhaps the best thing about wax for the beginner is that errors can be corrected. You can make a repair over and over until it is satisfactory. Don't like the looks of a repaired hole? Just dig the wax out and try again.

Matching the color of the wax filler to the color of the wood is the greatest problem. Wax sticks are available in a wide variety of colors and shades. Usually, however, you will have to mix colors to get a good match anyway, so you may as well get just a few stock colors.

U.S. Plywood, under its Weldwood brand name, offers individual "Blend-Sticks" in about twenty shades. The Magic Woodblend "Putty Pencil" comes in about fifteen shades. Minwax "Blend-Fil" pencils are available in a variety of colors. Even grocery and variety stores often have sets of four or six "furniture sticks." As a last choice you may use coloring crayons straight from the school supply or toy counter. Larger boxes of crayons contain several dark colors that are quite satisfactory on smaller defects.

Again, filler wax must not be used until the piece of furniture has been made its final color. Obviously, you cannot match a color that

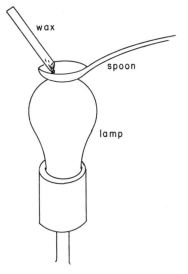

wax

spoon

lamp

MIXING WAX FILLER

has not yet been put on the wood. Filler wax may be used on pieces that are completely finished. So if your table is damaged by a falling knife, it is not necessary to strip it in order to repair it. On a piece that is being refinished, the proper time to use filler is after it has been stained but before the finish is applied.

Filling the hole and smoothing the surface is not difficult, but matching colors can be a little tricky. The larger the surface of the repair, the closer the match must be. A very small repair will blend in with normal variations in the wood unless the color is way off.

Sometimes you will have a wax stick that matches quite satisfactorily. Frequently, however, you will have to mix two or more waxes to achieve the right color. This mixing is done over a source of heat. A small bottle cap or a spoon can serve as a fine mixing bowl. Do not use a match or a candle for the heat source because they make soot that will throw the color off. You may use the kitchen stove, an inverted pressing iron, or even a soldering iron. We usually use a 100-watt lamp bulb.

A little of the wax, straight or mixed, is heated in a spoon over the bulb and then packed into the defect. The wax should be in a plastic state. If it has become a liquid, it is too hot and must be allowed to cool before use. A pocketknife blade or a curved X-acto blade is used to transfer the warm wax from spoon to hole and pack it in. When the surface of the wax is level with the surrounding wood, it must be smoothed over. You may prefer to do this by rubbing lightly with a fingertip, or you may use the blade. Sometimes it helps to warm the blade before the smoothing operation. The surface does not have to be perfect, since the finish will camouflage minor physical irregularities.

The color match must be good, however. Examine your completed work critically, close up and from a distance. If you can spot the repair easily, it is not good enough. In this case, scrape out the wax filler carefully and try again for a better match.

When you are satisfied with your wax stick repair, you may proceed to the finishing process *provided* it is oil, wax, or shellac. If the finish is to be varnish or lacquer, the wax repair *must* be sealed. It is extremely important that every bit of wax be sealed off from the varnish or lacquer that will be applied. The reason is that these finishes will react with any exposed wax and not dry properly.

Some wax stick sets include a small bottle identified as "sealer." This or very thin shellac—two parts alcohol to one part shellac—will adequately coat the repair. The sealer/shellac is brushed lightly but completely over all exposed wax. The edges should be feathered out on the wood to avoid an irregular surface. Shellac from a spray can is equally satisfactory for this use.

Occasionally, the refinisher is faced with a deep hole. It may extend completely through the board. If such a hole is large—say, the diameter of a pencil—wax filler should not be used alone. The bulk of this hole should be repaired with wood filler (see previous section). For reasons mentioned earlier, this filler must be topped off *below the level of the surrounding surface.* When the bulk wood filler is thoroughly dry, wax filler of the proper color is put on top of it to the level of the surface.

Though they occur infrequently, there are three situations in which wax stick repairs may prove unsatisfactory. Wax has a relatively low melting point and should not be used to repair pieces that will be subjected to high temperatures. Even moderate temperatures created by serving dishes on unprotected surfaces can soften wax to the point that it offers little physical support to the finish. Under these conditions the leg of a coffee server might puncture the finish. Perhaps one who mistreats a piece in this manner deserves what he gets. But such things do happen, and this type of damage (though not other damages from the excessive heat) can be prevented by using another filler material.

The second situation that may require a filler other than wax involves pressure. If a horizontal surface is to support heavy objects with relatively small feet, wax may not be sufficiently sturdy. Generally speaking, the larger the area of a horizontal repair, the more you should consider using another filler. Though size is not the only factor, a useful rule of thumb is not to use wax from penny-size up.

The last and most common condition for which wax is usually unsuitable is in rebuilding protruding corners. The corner of a table top, for example, is quite likely to be struck accidentally. A lasting repair should be harder than wax.

When you are faced with any of these situations, you may do one of two things. The repair may be made with wax filler, knowing that it may have to be redone from time to time. Of course, this will not mean restripping the piece. The repair is simply repaired and the finish in that area restored.

The second option in these cases is to use a filler substance harder than wax. This filler is known as "shellac sticks" and also comes in various colors and shades. Shellac sticks are much harder than wax sticks and they are more difficult to use. They require a much greater degree of skill if for no reason other than that it has to be done right the first time. Once in the hole, it is almost impossible to remove without causing further damage.

Shellac sticks are handled like wax: heated, mixed, and applied hot. The home refinisher who can handle wax stick repairs well can probably learn to use shellac sticks with a little practice on scrap boards. Shellac sticks are not for the beginner.

All is not lost if you are a beginner and you must have a shellac stick repair. You can have it done by a *good* professional refinisher. You can also have it done through a local furniture retailer.

A great deal of new furniture gets damaged in shipment and on showroom display. Larger stores have a person on the staff to repair such damage. Smaller establishments frequently make use of itinerant specialists who check in periodically. In either case, you can

REFINISHER'S PATHFINDER

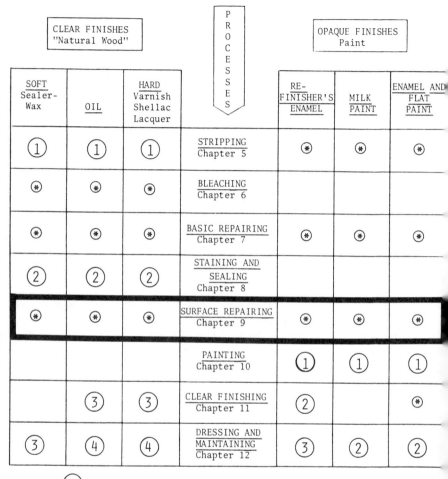

CLEAR FINISHES "Natural Wood"			PROCESSES	OPAQUE FINISHES Paint		
SOFT Sealer-Wax	OIL	HARD Varnish Shellac Lacquer		RE-FINISHER'S ENAMEL	MILK PAINT	ENAMEL AND FLAT PAINT
①	①	①	STRIPPING Chapter 5	✱	✱	✱
✱	✱	✱	BLEACHING Chapter 6			
✱	✱	✱	BASIC REPAIRING Chapter 7	✱	✱	✱
②	②	②	STAINING AND SEALING Chapter 8			
✱	✱	✱	SURFACE REPAIRING Chapter 9	✱	✱	✱
			PAINTING Chapter 10	①	①	①
	③	③	CLEAR FINISHING Chapter 11	②		✱
③	④	④	DRESSING AND MAINTAINING Chapter 12	③	②	②

① Necessary sequential processes
✱ Optional processes

probably arrange for him to make your repair in his off hours—for a fee, of course.

The Next Process

Your piece has now been stripped, sealed, stained, and repaired. It is ready for the application of the finish you have selected. The "Pathfinder" indicates the chapter containing the proper instructions.

10

Painting

Paint Characteristics

There is a wide variety of paint finishes. Those most useful to the refinisher will be discussed in detail in this chapter. First, let us consider the general characteristics and qualities of paint.

Of course, there is no one thing called "paint." Paint may be oil-based, water-based, or plastic-based. It may be fast-drying or slow. It may be glossy or flat. It may be tough or fragile. A paint may be any of these and more, but all paint has one common characteristic—it has color. Paint is opaque—that is, its color covers the surface on which it is applied so that the surface cannot be seen. When one looks at a painted surface, one sees the paint and not the hidden surface.

Paint is applied for the same reasons as any other finish—to protect the surface and to improve its appearance. Since all finishes protect the surface, some better and some worse than paint, this provides no reason for choosing paint over other types of finishes. Appearance, then, is the one reason for painting. As paint is opaque, it is chosen when the surface should be hidden from view. There are several circumstances that call for a paint finish.

At times the refinisher is faced with a piece that is damaged or scarred beyond concealed repair. If the repair (or replaced part) would be obvious under a clear finish, it would be best to paint the piece. While such defects are usually the result of accidents, they are occasionally the result of the work of inept refinishers. One such case involved an otherwise beautiful oak table that was brought in with a dozen one-inch plugs in the top. Someone had simply drilled out all the blemishes and inserted oak plugs. No effort had been made to match the grains of the plugs with the table top—in fact, most of the plugs were even inserted cross-grained. Repairing this mess would have been quite involved, so the owner, when informed of the cost, quite properly chose a paint finish to hide it all.

Another circumstance that dictates a paint finish is when a piece was painted originally. Contrary to what one would expect after looking through many "antique" shops today, many old pieces were painted when they were made. In early times, furniture makers often used different kinds of wood in a piece. Sometimes this was done because wood of different characteristics was needed for different uses; for example, one kind for a chair seat and another for an arched back. More often, however, the maker simply used whatever piece of wood happened to be closest to hand since it would be painted anyway.

At times paint was used to hide different types of wood in the same piece. On other occasions it was used just to provide relief from otherwise drab surroundings. Regardless of the reason for the original paint, purists will want such a piece refinished with paint.

A final reason for painting a piece of furniture is the most common. One wishes to make use of a piece of junk. A battered but useful chest is to be used for storage in playroom, shop, or garage. The utilitarian thing to do is to slap on a coat of paint and use it. The paint may be plain old enamel or flat or even one of those so-called "antiquing kits." It does not matter—the piece will look clean and not bad.

Paint finishes may be classified in many different ways. For our purposes we put them into three simple types: enamel and flat paint (including antiquing kits), refinisher's enamel, and milk paint. Each of these will be discussed in turn—enamel and flat paint for junk, refinisher's enamel for 95 percent of those pieces that should be painted, and milk paint for the special and unusual piece.

In spite of the repeated earlier warnings against the use of sandpaper, this is the one exception that proves the rule. Surfaces must be *smooth* before paint is applied. Since the surface under paint cannot be seen anyway, sandpaper may be used. In fact, it should be used on existing paint and varnish to provide a lightly scratched surface to which the new paint will adhere. Of course, all old wax has been removed with paint thinner. Needed surface repairs are made as detailed in Chapter 9. As with all finishes, we recommend the use of *new,* cheap brushes.

Enamel, Flat Paint, and Antiquing Kits

The finishes included in this section are the most commonly used and least desirable paint finishes for furniture. They do seal and protect the surfaces to which applied. They are easy to apply and they can produce a pleasing appearance.

They do have several disadvantages. Flat paint is just that: *flat.* Only in the most extraordinary circumstances can it be used alone as *the* finish on a piece. (It is, however, quite valuable in combination with other finishes. See Refinisher's Enamel below.) The dead dullness of this finish removes it from serious consideration here.

Enamel has two major strikes against its use on good furniture. The more minor problem is that it cannot be repaired. Scratches, chips, and cracks can be covered with a spot of the same color *if* the original paint has not faded. Even if the color match is perfect, the result looks spotted. The reason for this is that enamel cannot be changed in any way after it is dry. That is the second and more serious problem in the use of enamel; the way it dries is the way it must remain.

It is almost impossible to apply enamel with a brush and not leave brush marks. These marks (and any others that dry in the finish) *cannot be removed.* Enamel cannot be smoothed in any manner. Steel wool, sandpaper, pumice, or any type of abrasive agent produces a scratched, blotchy surface. An enamel finish must be made as near perfect as possible while it is wet because nothing further can be done once it starts drying.

If enamel must be used, best (but not good) results can be had by following these steps.

First, paint one surface of the piece at a time, starting with the uppermost and proceeding downward. Second, if possible turn the piece so that the surface being painted is horizontal. Third, slop the enamel on the working surface quickly and evenly, brushing in any and every direction. Fourth, "tip off" the wet enamel by brushing in one direction only, using just the tips of the bristles with the brush held at a right angle to the surface. Fifth, and finally, *leave the surface alone*—the more you fool with it, the worse it will look.

Of course, enamel may be sprayed, but satisfactory results demand good spray equipment (about $100 minimum investment) and a very skilled hand. These are unavailable to the amateur and unnecessary for the professional. Fortunately, there is refinisher's enamel for both.

Antiquing (kits) requires the application of two or more paints. The first, called "ground color," is applied evenly over the entire piece. The second may be applied evenly over the dried ground color and then roughly wiped off with a rag. Either way, the result is a piece of ground color with the accent color dabbed into corners and crevices. One kit manufacturer even provides a gritty, dirtlike substance to scatter around in the wet paint. If you insist on trying this type of finish, just follow the directions in the kit. You can't go wrong. Directions or no, you will end up with a mess—the only result achievable with one of these "messing kits."

Refinisher's Enamel

In spite of all that has been said, there is a good opaque finish that comes in any desired degree of gloss and is easy to apply. It is known by a number of different names, all of which are probably unknown at the local paint store. This finish cannot be bought; you will have to "roll your own." We call it "refinisher's enamel" because it is used almost exclusively by professional refinishers who do quality work.

Refinisher's enamel is really a combination of two finishes: flat paint and varnish (or shellac). It has all the advantages of regular enamel without its drawbacks. Refinisher's enamel *can* be abraded for smoothness and spot-free repairing. Therein lies its great value to the pros.

The color and opaqueness of this finish is provided by the flat paint. The protective hardness and desired degree of gloss is provided by the overcoating of varnish. The perfection of this finish is possible because it does not have to be left as it comes from the brush. Refinisher's enamel looks like regular enamel, only better. It is the only opaque finish that we recommend other than milk paint (See below).

The first step in this process is to apply a coat of flat paint of the desired color. This is done in the normal manner: smooth surface, quick but even coating of paint, and "tipping off" with the bristles vertical to the surface. The paint may be oil- or water-based, though we generally prefer the latter for ease of mixing, toning, and applying.

This coat of flat paint will show at least a few inevitable brush marks when it is dry. These and any other imperfections such as dust or lint that settled before it dried are simply removed by rubbing the surface with fine steel wool. Grade 3/0 or 4/0 is all that is generally required. More than one coat of flat paint may be required but not normally unless a dark surface is being covered with a light color.

After smoothing with steel wool, the surface(s) should be cleaned carefully of steel and dust particles. Our regular procedure is to vacuum the entire piece and then wipe it with a cloth dampened in mineral spirits (paint thinner).

The piece is now ready for the application of the second half of the finish: a coat of varnish. Details of this operation are found in Chapter 11.

The superiority of refinisher's enamel to regular enamel must be seen to be believed. It *is* worth the slight extra work required.

Milk Paint

"Milk paint" is the name given to that paint used in the early days of this country, the main ingredient of which was milk. Though this type of finish is an anachronism today, it is used to restore and refinish those few pieces that one finds with an original milk-paint finish.

Milk paint is a very tough opaque finish. In effect, it is more like a coating of glue than paint. Ordinary paint and varnish removers will not touch it, though it can be stripped (see Chapter 5). One generally finds it today under other finishes and recognizes it because the remover stops working on reaching it.

In the early days, milk paint was made with whole milk to which color was added. The "color" was usually blood, clay, or berry juice. Fortunately, we can make our own milk paint with less exotic ingredients.

Dehydrated milk powder or crystals is mixed with water until it has the consistency of paint. This may be used "as is" for a white finish, or it may be colored first. A wide variety of colors is available as a dry powder at larger paint stores. These may be mixed to any desired hue in the dry form or added, one at a time, directly to the milk paint. Mixing color for an entire piece presents no problem, but attempting to match an existing color can require a great deal of experimentation.

Milk paint is brushed on just like the more familiar types of paint. After drying, it should be allowed to set for several days before abrading in any way.

REFINISHER'S PATHFINDER

SOFT Sealer-Wax	OIL	HARD Varnish Shellac Lacquer	PROCESSES	RE-FINISHER'S ENAMEL	MILK PAINT	ENAMEL AND FLAT PAINT
①	①	①	STRIPPING Chapter 5	✱	✱	✱
✱	✱	✱	BLEACHING Chapter 6			
✱	✱	✱	BASIC REPAIRING Chapter 7	✱	✱	✱
②	②	②	STAINING AND SEALING Chapter 8			
✱	✱	✱	SURFACE REPAIRING Chapter 9	✱	✱	✱
			PAINTING Chapter 10	①	①	①
	③	③	CLEAR FINISHING Chapter 11	②		✱
③	④	④	DRESSING AND MAINTAINING Chapter 12	③	②	②

Column headers above are grouped: CLEAR FINISHES "Natural Wood" (SOFT Sealer-Wax, OIL, HARD Varnish Shellac Lacquer); OPAQUE FINISHES Paint (RE-FINISHER'S ENAMEL, MILK PAINT, ENAMEL AND FLAT PAINT)

① Necessary sequential processes
✱ Optional processes

The Next Process

Refinishers, amateur and professional alike, seldom have a need to apply paint finishes. Nearly all furniture, both old and new, has a clear finish today. Even those pieces that were originally painted are usually refinished clear.

Though there is less painting than probably should be, there is enough to require every refinisher to know how to paint. We strongly recommend against the use of enamel or "antiquing" on any piece. Refinisher's enamel will meet about 95 percent of one's paint needs. Milk paint will meet the remainder.

Those readers who have applied enamel or milk paint should turn to Chapter 12, "Dressing and Maintaining." Those who are applying refinisher's enamel should proceed to Chapter 11, "Clear Finishing."

11

Clear Finishing

Choosing the Finish

The proper application of the finish—protective coating—is one of the most important processes in the entire refinishing procedure. The project piece of furniture has been stripped, stained, sealed, and perhaps bleached and repaired. The clear finish that will now be applied may accentuate the beauty of the piece, or do nothing for it, or seriously detract from it. In any instance, the outcome will be determined by the skill of the refinisher in choosing the type of clear finish and in applying it. Information on which the choice was made was given in detail earlier (Chapter 4), and it will be reviewed here. Skill in applying clear finishes will be improved by following the instructions in this chapter, which will consider in turn the soft, hard, and oil finishes.

The beginning refinisher should be aware after reading preceding chapters that, though he earlier chose the type of finish for the piece, there are some options still open. Only if a linseed oil finish has been prepared for must he partially retrace his steps in order to use one of the other clear finishes. In this case, the wood must be sealed, and shellac must be the first finish coat applied. In other cases, the refinisher may yet change his mind as the preparation has been compatible. He may freely interchange the sealer-wax, varnish, shellac, lacquer, and antique oil finishes.

To avoid confusion for those who may have misread the "Pathfinder," it should be restated that the soft clear finish (sealer-wax) is not included in this chapter. This finish is achieved simply by applying a good wax dressing to the sealer-stain applied earlier. These instructions are found in Chapter 12.

The Hard Clear Finishes

The hard clear finishes consist of varnish, shellac, and lacquer. Their characteristics are summarized and compared in the following charts.

Characteristics During Application

FINISH	BRUSH ON	AFFECTED BY WAX	AFFECTED BY HUMIDITY	DRYING TIME
Varnish	Yes	Yes	No	Longest
Shellac	Yes	No	Yes	Middle
Lacquer	Difficult	Yes	Yes	Shortest

Characteristics After Drying

FINISH	HARDNESS	DEPTH (THICKNESS)	WATERPROOF	ALCOHOLPROOF
Varnish	Hardest	Middle	Yes	Yes
Shellac	Harder	Greatest	No	No
Lacquer	Hard	Least	No	No

Among the several interesting facts that emerge from these charts, two stand out. The long drying time of varnish clearly indicates why it is all but impossible to purchase new furniture with that finish. The other superior characteristics of varnish give sufficient reason why quality cabinetmakers and refinishers prefer it to all others.

The preparation of the piece for any of the three hard finishes is the same. After the application of sealer-stain and the repair of surface defects, if any, every surface must be steel-wooled thoroughly. Grade 2/0 (00) steel wool must be rubbed briskly with the grain in order to remove minor surface irregularities. Finally, the piece must be cleaned of all particles and dust with a dry cloth, brush, and vacuum cleaner. Any particles that remain can be depended on to mar the finish. The piece is now ready for any of the three hard finishes.

VARNISH

The materials needed for the application of a varnish finish are a portable light, a brush, grades 3/0 and 4/0 steel wool, and a can of varnish. The portable light may be dispensed with if the project piece is small and easily movable; however, even then it is a great convenience. The light is used to cause a reflection on the surface being finished. It is placed on the opposite side of the piece from the refinisher so that the light is reflected on the varnish as it is applied. This is the best method for preventing missed places or "holidays" in the coat. Without a light in the proper position it is extremely difficult to be sure that there are no gaps in the application. Even very small holidays that are discovered immediately necessitate another complete coat of finish. Of course, the light or the piece must be moved to the proper position for each new work surface.

The type of brush used is critical to the success of a varnish finish. The amateur refinisher should *not* purchase a "varnish" brush. These brushes are both expensive and very difficult to handle. Even we do not use them. Instead, we use the same type of brush we use for stripping. These are, of course, the cheapest 2″ and 2½″ brushes such as are available in discount and variety stores for thirty to fifty cents each. There are several reasons for recommending that you use the same.

Varnish, as well as shellac and lacquer, must be applied with a brush that is absolutely clean. Thoroughly cleaning a brush after use is a time-consuming process that requires cleaner and patience. Obviously, new brushes are clean, so we use one each time. After it has been used once for varnishing, the brush is swished around in some remover, then used in the stripping process as long as it lasts.

Strangely enough, it is actually easier for the amateur to apply a good coat of varnish with one of these cheap brushes than with one that is made for the purpose. We will discuss technique shortly. The disadvantage of these brushes is that they do shed more bristles than the more expensive brushes. However, fanning the bristles back and forth across outstretched fingers several times will reduce this problem, and those that do shed while varnishing are as easily removed as those that shed from varnish brushes.

The varnish itself is another matter. The cheapest is not the best. First, however, *under no circumstances should you buy "spar" varnish for refinishing furniture.* Spar varnish is a marine product that has its uses but not on furniture. Spar varnish is especially prepared so that it never thoroughly dries to a hard finish. If you have ever sat on "tacky" wooden furniture, you were probably sitting on spar varnish. The only remedy for such mistakes is to return to the stripping process and begin again. The *wrong* can states: SPAR or MARINE. The *right* can states: for FURNITURE or FLOORS.

After trying many brands, we have settled on McCloskey brand Heirloom varnish because it has so many of the desirable characteristics. McCloskey's is relatively inexpensive and comes in four degrees of gloss: eggshell, satin, semi-gloss, and gloss. The latter characteristic saves the refinisher a great deal of work, as you will see later. Heirloom varnish is readily obtainable, easy to apply, and has excellent keeping qualities. And that brings us to the point of slaying another dragon.

There are those experts who caution the amateur that he should never keep varnish after the can has been opened. One is advised to throw away the can and remaining contents after a single use and open a new one for the next piece. We can only say that we have not encountered this problem. After using from a can we replace the top tightly with a rubber hammer and repeatedly reopen it and brush away. If, after several weeks of storage, there should be a hardened layer on top of the varnish, this should be taken out carefully *in one piece* with a stirring paddle. As long as small pieces of this skim do not get loose in the varnish we have found absolutely no difference in the brushing, drying, or hardness characteristics. Even if the storage time runs to several months and the varnish is unusable, you have lost nothing by trying.

Heirloom varnish has a spirit base and, therefore, may be used over the Minwax brand stains we prefer. You will recall from Chapter 8 that only varnish with a spirit base may be used with this stain (though, of course, shellac may be used also).

There are other brands of varnish the amateur refinisher will find to be satisfactory. You may wish to try several and settle on the one that suits your needs.

We have not found the urethane or plastic varnishes to be very satisfactory for use by the home refinisher. They do produce an extremely tough finish, but they are difficult to apply. Brush marks are frequently a problem with urethane varnish, and if they dry in the finish, you are stuck with them unless you back up and strip it all off. A further disadvantage of this type of varnish is that it is very high-gloss. Since we seldom desire a high-gloss finish, we must do a lot of work on it to tone it down.

Now we come to the actual application of the varnish, which works best in temperatures around 70 degrees. The room should be clean, relatively dust-free, and well ventilated. (Varnishing outdoors is not recommended because blowing debris is likely to ruin the finish before it dries.) The piece is turned so that the work surface is horizontal if possible. The light is positioned on the opposite side to reflect on that surface. The new brush is fanned and all is ready.

Varnish is used straight from the can. No thinning should be done even though the label says that it *can* be thinned. (Of course, it must be thinned if it is to be used in a spray gun.)

We prefer to begin most pieces upside down in order to finish the underside first. With a small or medium table, for example, varnish the underside of the top and the legs and stretchers before turning it upright, leaving a small area unvarnished to serve as a handle. Most refinishers find this method more convenient than leaving the piece upright and working upside down.

One surface—a top, a side, a leg, or a drawer front—should be done at a time. Each should be completed before another is begun. As indicated earlier, every surface that can be reached should be varnished. Though it is never seen, even the underside of the top of a chest, for example, should have a protective coating in order to moisture-seal the wood and minimize shrinkage.

With the surface between you and the light, varnish is quickly applied to the entire surface with an adequately loaded brush (if varnish drips off the brush, it is too loaded). Brushing hard in any and every direction coats every part of the surface with varnish.

The light reflection should be checked to be sure that no "holidays" have been left. If not, the varnish coat is smoothed out by using just the tips of the bristles and brushing over the entire surface in the direction of the grain.

Any brush marks that remain after tipping may be disregarded, as most will disappear as the varnish dries. Any others will be taken care of with steel wool and dressing. Once a surface has been tipped off, *it must not be touched again* until it is thoroughly dry (twelve to twenty-four hours). This same procedure is followed on one surface after another until the piece is complete. That's really all there is to varnishing except for a few special techniques that may save you some trouble.

Varnish will run just like other liquids. If it is applied too heavily, or if it is unevenly applied, it will run on vertical surfaces—especially out of corners and crevices. It will not take long to get the feel of how much is too much. You can minimize the problem by turning the piece so that each surface is horizontal while you are working on it. There will be runs, however, and they can be removed with the tip of the brush *while wet.* Just stand around with the brush and good lighting and barely tip the blobs as they appear. Those that are not found until they have started to dry should be left alone. After drying, they can be shaved off carefully with a razor knife or razor blade and smoothed with steel wool.

A finish will seldom, if ever, dry at a uniform rate. For this reason, a surface will often appear blotched or streaked when partially dry. Resist the temptation to touch-up a little. Even if you do see an actual "holiday," nothing can be done about it at this time without causing further damage. Once drying has begun, the only cure for a missed spot is another coat. This does not necessarily mean that the entire piece needs a second coat. Since varnish does not "build up," only one surface can be recoated with no difference in the appearance.

A wooden drawer knob can present quite a problem until you discover that it can be held by a partially inserted screw when applying varnish. Inserting the screw in the top of a soft-drink bottle provides an ideal place for a knob to dry.

Most varieties of varnish will feel dry to the touch in a few hours. We advise you, however, to play it safe. Allow each coat to dry at least twenty-four hours. Drying time does vary with environmental conditions, and you certainly don't want to ruin all your previous work by allowing insufficient drying time.

It may be advisable to apply a second varnish coat. While the application of unneeded coats of finish is usually wasted time and effort, there are some circumstances that require the application of two. If the intended use of the piece makes it necessary for it to be absolutely water and alcoholproof, we recommend two coats of varnish. Two coats are no more waterproof than one coat; but we use a second coat on the tops only of tables and serving boards, for example, as insurance just in case we missed one or two minute spots with the first coat. Three coats of varnish is a waste of time, and even two on the legs and other vertical surfaces is completely unnecessary. The second coat of varnish makes no change in the appearance of the finish. You do not get more gloss or a build-up with additional coats of varnish. Our standard practice consists of one over-all coat, followed by a second coat on the tops of tables, chests, and serving pieces. We, and now you, can deviate from this when special needs exist.

Whatever the number of coats being applied, it is necessary to use steel wool between each. Brisk rubbing with 3/0 or 4/0 steel wool serves the dual purpose of removing irregularities and of providing a "tooth" to help hold the following coat. Use 3/0 to lessen the gloss and 4/0 to add gloss. The most practical method is choosing the varnish with the specific gloss desired and using grade 3/0 steel wool exclusively. Whether you plan a second coat or not, hard rubbing with the steel wool in the direction of the grain is necessary.

The desired amount of gloss is best achieved by choosing the varnish that produces it, but we sometimes make mistakes or change our minds.

If you are not satisfied with the degree of gloss, adjustments may be made on the final coat, allowing for the fact that the wax dressing will increase the gloss slightly. Gloss may be "toned down" by rubbing with 3/0 steel wool. The result will be satin or even dull, depending on how much the surface is rubbed. On the other hand, the degree of gloss is increased by using 4/0 steel wool. In either case, care must be taken not to rub so ferociously as to cut through the finish. Exposed edges and corners are particularly susceptible to this treatment.

Shellac is most often used for one of two reasons: It builds depth or body of finish rather quickly, and it may be used over wax. When building body, the refinisher uses one, two, or three coats of shellac, which he frequently tops with a coat of varnish for its additional toughness and waterproof characteristics. When dealing with a very intricate surface from which he may not have removed the last vestige of wax, or a surface with wax patches, the refinisher applies a first coat of shellac.

Shellac is not only discolored by water after it is dry but it will dry discolored (cloudy) if it is applied in a high-humidity environment. The best protection against this happening to your piece is to *not* apply shellac when it is raining or even on a muggy day. Should this misfortune befall you, it may be overcome by using the restoring trick discussed in Chapter 13, but you will probably end up stripping the piece again.

We have found no significant difference in shellac from one brand to another. You may select the one that is most readily available, just being sure that it is brushing rather than spraying shellac (once more: *read the label*).

The technique for applying shellac is like that described for varnish in the preceding section with one important exception. Shellac dries faster than varnish, so the refinisher must work more rapidly to get an even coat, and runs should be spotted sooner. Thinned with denatured alcohol, shellac will be easier to apply, but it does not build as much depth.

The degree of gloss is not easily controlled. It is very difficult to acquire satin or dull gloss with shellac. A rougher grade of steel wool is recommended between coats: grade 2/0. Shellac dries in about two hours, but allow six hours between coats. If an overcoat of varnish is to be applied, the shellac should be rubbed briskly with 2/0 steel wool. Shellac can be used later if the container is closed tightly. Test on scrap wood before using.

Because of its inferior characteristics, we do not recommend lacquer for the home refinisher. The beginner, especially, will have great difficulty with its application. If you must use lacquer, spray it on. Considerable practice is needed before attempting to apply it to a good piece of furniture. Jumping into lacquer is a good way to get practice at restripping!

Thin, fast-drying lacquer in convenient spray cans does have its use in restoring. This use is discussed in Chapter 13.

Oil Finishes

As has been pointed out earlier (Chapter 4), a good oil finish is undoubtedly the most beautiful one for fine antiques. It provides a depth and beauty that can only be approached with finishes of other types. For many years linseed oil was used in a long and back-breaking process. While linseed oil may still be used by the purist, Minwax brand Antique Oil Finish will produce the same result in a fraction of the time. Instructions for both processes will be discussed.

LINSEED OIL

The linseed oil finish may be applied to any piece that has been stained but not sealed. In Chapter 8 we recommended an oil-penetrating stain for these pieces. This finishing process is not complicated.

First, be sure to obtain the right kind of linseed oil. The brand does not matter, but the type must be *boiled*. Both "raw" and "boiled" linseed oil are readily available. The raw oil never dries and therefore cannot be used on furniture. Check the label and be sure that you purchase *boiled* linseed oil. (Incidentally, do *not* attempt to boil raw linseed oil.)

For use, linseed oil is thinned about three parts oil to one part paint thinner (mineral spirits). This is applied very liberally with a brush or soft cloth to the entire piece, which is then placed in an out-of-the-way corner where it will stay for several weeks. The idea is for the wood to absorb its fill of oil, so it must be checked every day or so, with more oil applied to any areas that appear to be drying. This phase continues for an unpredictable length of time, depending on the type and dryness of the wood and the temperature. You will know that it has gone on long enough only when the wood appears to be taking no more oil. The piece is wiped of as much oil as possible with soft rags, allowed to dry for three weeks, and then phase two begins.

After three weeks for drying, a very thin film of the thinned oil is rubbed into all surfaces of the piece, and it is allowed to dry for another two or three weeks, after which time the treatment is repeated. This phase—oil, dry, oil, dry, and so on—is continued for at least four or five months. If at any time the slightest stickiness is found, the drying time between oil applications must be increased.

This linseed-oil process simply cannot be speeded up effectively. Warmer temperatures will hasten the absorbing and drying times somewhat, but five or six months is about the best that one can do. Of course, the longer phase two is continued, the more depth and beauty there is to the linseed-oil finish. Only the finest of antiques, however, are worthy of this difficult process.

MINWAX ANTIQUE OIL

The Minwax Company has an outstanding product called Antique Oil Finish, which produces a beautiful oil finish in a few days. We recommend it to the beginner and to the experienced refinisher. We have not applied a linseed-oil finish since discovering it (though, of course, linseed oil is still used occasionally in restoring). The application of Minwax Antique Oil Finish is straightforward though somewhat strenuous.

Over Minwax stain (Chapter 8) a heavy coat of Antique Oil is applied with a soft cloth. In a few minutes when it appears to be drying, the surface is buffed with a cloth or a hand-held buffer. Twenty-four hours later the process is repeated and the piece is ready to use. Obviously, there is no comparison between the application time of six months for linseed oil and just a few days for an Antique Oil Finish.

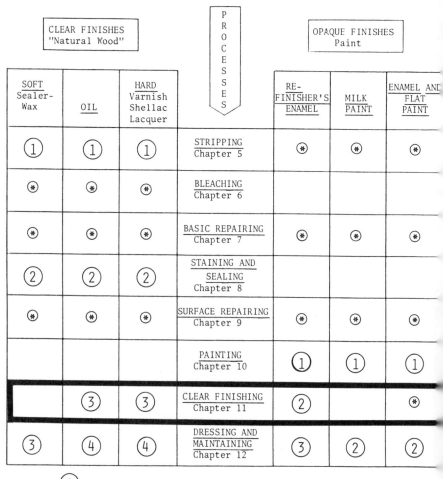

① Necessary sequential processes
⊛ Optional processes

The Next Process

While any piece of furniture may be used immediately after the finish is dry, this would make it difficult to maintain the original appearance. In order to protect the finish, beautify it, and facilitate maintenance, the piece is dressed (waxed). The exception to this statement, of course, is the oil finish, which requires a special maintenance procedure. Complete directions on dressing and maintaining all types of finishes will be found in Chapter 12.

12

Dressing and Maintaining

Dressing

Dressing is the final process in refinishing a piece before it is put into use. This is nothing more than the application of a good wax coating. All furniture should be dressed prior to use. Incidentally, new furniture from factory or showroom and furniture refinished in the typical shop is usually not dressed when delivered to the home. The purchaser should dress such pieces as soon as they are received. There are several reasons for putting a good coat of wax on every hard finish—varnish, shellac, lacquer, and paint. Even marble should be dressed with wax. Wax is not used on oil finishes, of course.

First, dressing adds to the beauty of the finish. The coating of wax increases the apparent depth and richness of the finish. Further, it minimizes slight blemishes and imperfections that may exist in the finish. Wax produces a smoothness that is difficult to achieve in any other way.

On the more practical side, the dressing adds to the durability of the finish. The dried and hardened wax provides a measure of physical protection to the finish and thus to the wood itself. In addition, though it is *not* waterproof, a good dressing may be called water-resistant. It delays the moisture from reaching the wood or finish that is not waterproof and allows more time to wipe moisture off before it causes damage.

Now it should be obvious why we advised against a sealer-wax finish except in very unusual circumstances. With only sealer/stain and wax on the wood, it has little protection against wear and almost none against accidents. You have done practically all the work of a good refinishing job, but your piece has no real protective coating. Before putting the wax dressing on the sealer/stain, we urge you to reconsider the little extra work involved in first applying a coat of varnish, shellac, or even lacquer.

While the dressing process can be omitted, we strongly recommend that every refinished (and new) piece be dressed. Initially, the wax will increase the gloss slightly, but this wears down in a few weeks as the piece is dusted.

Many available dressing products that promise miracles create only confusion. There is only one type of wax to use on furniture, and that is a *good paste* wax. We prefer Minwax Paste Finishing Wax. Johnson's Paste Wax runs a very close second in our opinion. We use no liquid or spray waxes or polishes. Minwax Paste Finishing Wax can be found in paint and hardware stores that carry Minwax products. Johnson's Paste Wax can be found on the grocery-store shelf.

Paste wax is recommended for several reasons. Dirt and dust will not cling to paste wax as they do to other types of waxes and polishes. In addition to causing furniture to darken more quickly with accumulated dirt, a liquid or spray wax or polish has the added disadvantage of requiring more frequent application. Spray and liquid products provide little or no protection to the finish. These should never be applied over paste wax.

Paste wax is applied according to the directions on the can. Two light coats are superior to one heavy coat. The second coat may be applied immediately after the first is buffed. This simple procedure produces a quality dressing that is easy to maintain.

Maintenance of Dressings

Apart from normal dusting with a soft dry cloth, it is desirable to run over the dressed surfaces with a damp cloth periodically. This prevents dirt from grinding into the wax or the finish. A briskly applied dry cloth will restore the shine.

At intervals of approximately twelve months, a new wax dressing should be applied. The timing will vary depending on the amount of use the piece receives.

To redress, first the piece should be thoroughly cleaned with a damp cloth and *mild* soap. This is followed by a plain damp cloth. Then the surface is immediately wiped dry. This removes the particles of dust and dirt that may have become embedded in the wax; it does not remove the wax. After the piece is thoroughly dry, a thin coat of paste wax is used to redress the piece. This maintenance program will provide many years of service from well-finished furniture.

After a very considerable time there may appear an objectionable wax build-up that mars the true beauty of the finish. Such a build-up is removed by cleaning the surfaces with a soft clean cloth soaked in paint thinner. Paint thinner is available in many brands. There is no significant difference among them. Just ask the clerk for paint thinner. Paint thinner (mineral spirits) will completely remove dirt, grease, and old wax without harming the finish. When the cleaned surface is dry, it is only necessary to dress the piece as was done originally. This process may be done as often as desired but is not necessary more than every other year even on hard used pieces.

Maintenance of Oil Finishes

As mentioned earlier, oil finishes are *not* dressed with wax. In a sense, the oil is both a finish and a dressing. This, too, must be maintained whether it is Minwax Antique Oil or linseed oil.

Oil finishes (remember that they are not oily to the touch) are dusted in the normal fashion: wiped lightly with a clean, dry soft cloth. No wax or polish is used.

Periodic cleaning of oil finishes is required. This should be done every six to twelve months, depending on usage of the piece. Mild soap and water will be satisfactory in normal circumstances. When thoroughly dry, the piece should be reoiled with one application of Minwax Antique Oil or linseed, whichever was used originally.

Neglected or very heavily used pieces may require a more thorough cleaning. In such cases, substitute paint thinner for the soap and water in the above procedure.

Marble

A number of people seem to have a fear that caring for marble is very difficult. This is not the case. Marble is dressed with good paste wax just as is wood finish. It is cleaned with mild soap and water and, when thoroughly dry, redressed with a light coat of paste wax.

It is true that marble is sometimes stained or even etched by substances spilled on it. While the same is true of wood, stains are often more noticeable on marble because of the lighter color. Then, too, marble is more often placed into use without a proper dressing to help protect it. To make matters even worse, thoughtless people will put things on a marble tabletop that they would not dream of placing on fine wood.

The stain-producing substance should be removed as soon as possible after a mishap. Frequently, the longer it stays on the marble, the more difficult it is to remove. Stains of unknown origin must often be attacked with one remover after another until the right one is found. Soap and water should be tried first on the chance that this simple remedy will suffice. Common household substances as well as commercial preparations may be tried, as indicated below. Any chemical should be used with care and according to instructions. Special care should be taken to protect any adjoining wood surfaces.

ORGANIC STAINS

Stains of an organic nature, such as coffee, tea, cosmetics, and juice, are removed with hydrogen peroxide (hair-bleaching strength at the drugstore) or full-strength household ammonia.

Wash the marble to remove all surface dirt. Apply a white paper towel or napkin soaked with straight hydrogen peroxide directly to the stain. This is called a poultice. Cover the poultice with a piece of glass or plastic to slow evaporation. Stains will usually disappear in an hour. The process is repeated as necessary.

All traces of the peroxide must be washed off the marble. Dry thoroughly and apply paste wax.

Ammonia is used to remove stains before they penetrate the surface. Mix one-half cup of ammonia with one quart of water. Apply to the stain with a soft cloth. Rinse well with warm water. If the stain remains, other mentioned procedures will be necessary.

OIL STAINS

Stains caused by peanut butter, dairy products, or any oil-base products usually have dark centers with lighter shades toward the edges.

Apply a poultice soaked in amyl acetate or acetone. Leave the poultice until it is dry, then rinse the surface with warm water. Dry thoroughly with a clean cloth and dress.

RUST STAINS

Rust stains caused from flower pots and metal objects can be removed with a commercial rust remover. Follow directions on the container. To prevent the harsh chemicals in rust removers from etching marble, it is imperative to work quickly and remove all traces with water immediately. When dry, apply paste wax.

PAINT OR PAINT STAINS

It is safe to use paint remover on marble. The surface may become darkened, but it can be easily bleached with the hydrogen-peroxide treatment.

Remove as much paint as possible with a razor blade. Cover the area with a poultice soaked with paint remover. Remove the poultice after five minutes and wipe away any remaining paint. Rinse well

REFINISHER'S PATHFINDER

SOFT Sealer-Wax	OIL	HARD Varnish Shellac Lacquer	PROCESSES	RE-FINISHER'S ENAMEL	MILK PAINT	ENAMEL AND FLAT PAINT
①	①	①	STRIPPING Chapter 5	✳	✳	✳
✳	✳	✳	BLEACHING Chapter 6			
✳	✳	✳	BASIC REPAIRING Chapter 7	✳	✳	✳
②	②	②	STAINING AND SEALING Chapter 8			
✳	✳	✳	SURFACE REPAIRING Chapter 9	✳	✳	✳
			PAINTING Chapter 10	①	①	①
	③	③	CLEAR FINISHING Chapter 11	②		✳
③	④	④	DRESSING AND MAINTAINING Chapter 12	③	②	②

CLEAR FINISHES "Natural Wood"

OPAQUE FINISHES Paint

① Necessary sequential processes
✳ Optional processes

with warm water. Repeat the procedure until all paint is removed. Dry thoroughly and apply paste wax.

These marks are removed by a process that in effect sands the marble smooth. Wet the surface just around the mark. Sprinkle with the powder of a suitable commercial preparation or tin oxide that can be found in hardware stores. Rub with a damp cloth until the surface is smooth and shiny. Rinse thoroughly with water, dry the surface, and apply paste wax.

Metals

Commercial cleaners give satisfactory results for normal cleaning of brass and other metals. Full-strength household ammonia applied and rubbed gently with grade 00 steel wool cleans badly tarnished brass.

Metal and brass pieces such as hinges and escutcheons should be coated with varnish, shellac, or lacquer for lasting protection against tarnish.

Summary

The application of a good dressing is the final step in refinishing. Except for oil finishes, every piece, both wood and marble, should have the protection of a dressing. Furniture with a good finish and a good dressing can be used with little fear of surface damage.

A proper maintenance program will provide many years of service from furniture. Maintenance, as explained in this chapter, is easily accomplished. It greatly extends the usefulness of a piece before major effort is required to recondition it.

13

Restoring Old Finishes

This chapter might have been entitled "Repairing Old Finishes." To restore is simply to clean up and to repair—to return an old finish to the original condition or better. Restoring is *not* refinishing, which includes stripping.

It is obvious that every old piece can be refinished. Any old piece is a candidate for restoring if some of the original finish remains. Then the "restore or refinish" decision must be made. At times this decision can be a difficult one. Influencing factors were discussed in some detail in Chapter 2 and will not be repeated here. The beginner is reminded only that the restore-refinish decision is based on the nature, age, value, and condition of the piece and its remaining finish.

Further, it should be kept in mind that restoring a finish requires much less time and effort than a complete refinishing job. Other things being equal, the refinisher always opts for restoring. Restored finishes can often be so effective that unscrupulous "operators" will pass off a restoring job as refinishing and charge accordingly. Restorations can be that good.

Home refinishers will sometimes restore for a special reason. This occurs when a piece cannot be refinished right after purchase. It may be quickly and temporarily restored so that it can be used until refinishing is convenient. Several pieces may be purchased together and the better ones given a quick restoration for use while the worst are being refinished.

Whatever the reasons, you have before you a piece that you have decided to restore rather than refinish. This chapter will *not* provide all the information you will need to do the job.

Restoring old finishes is not a "process." In reality it is all the processes discussed in the preceding chapters. There is no such person as a "furniture restorer." The *refinisher* uses his regular processes and procedures in restoring. He may and often does modify those procedures, but they are refinishing procedures. This fact makes it difficult for the beginner to restore old finishes.

Restoring finishes requires a good knowledge of the refinishing processes. We urge the beginner to gain such knowledge by studying thoroughly Chapters 5 through 12. Certainly he will have to refer back to them while working with restoring instructions. The best course of action for the beginner, however, is to do some refinishing before attempting a restoring project. If you have a piece to restore, we suggest that you set it aside and refinish one or two other pieces first.

On the other hand, the beginner can do no *real* harm if he decides to jump right into a restoration project. Should things not work out satisfactorily, the piece can be completely refinished at any stage. Lost: some time, some effort, and possibly some value in rare cases of original finishes with intrinsic worth.

Cleaning the Piece

The newcomer to furniture refinishing will often be astonished by the results of a simple but thorough cleaning of a piece. Gold is not only found under "them thar hills," but it may be found under dirt and wax. The sheer quantity of dirt and wax and dirt and polish and dirt and gunk that can accumulate on a piece of furniture in twenty years—to say nothing of fifty or two hundred—is beyond belief. Removing this mess is the first step in restoring an old finish.

Thorough cleaning of the piece is essential. Proper cleaning removes the dirt, wax, and polish without harming whatever finish is beneath it. This is done with paint thinner (mineral spirits). Soap and water will not do the job. Steel wool does too much; it will get into the finish, too. In any case, thinner will do the job better and easier.

A note of caution: Paint thinner will not harm any *normal* finish. Sometimes the ancients used *ab*normal finishes, even of their individual concoction. You may wish to try it on a small inconspicuous area first. However, if you do run across some weird finish, you probably will have to refinish the piece finally.

A clean soft cloth is moistened with paint thinner and rubbed briskly on the surface to be cleaned. In cases of extreme accumulations, it will be necessary to repeat this operation several times. Clean the *entire* piece in this manner—top, bottom, sides, inside, and outside. Change cloths frequently and keep at it until the cloth is no longer discolored by the removed wax and dirt.

When the piece is completely clean, you should examine it carefully. Now you can really determine just how much of the original finish remains. Note the bad places that cleared up with the cleaning. Look for damaged finish (and wood) that was revealed by cleaning.

This is the time for a final commitment to restore or strip. It is not that you can't stop restoring at any time and strip the piece, but to do so later will waste considerable time and effort. On marginal pieces, the restore-refinish decision rears its ugly head for re-evaluation every step of the way.

Match-Staining

Your careful examination may disclose some areas of wear down into the wood. Such areas frequently are worn down beyond the original stain, making them lighter than surrounding surfaces. This requires staining to match the worn and unworn areas. Match-staining can prove very difficult to accomplish.

If the worn area is large or if there are many of them, you should give consideration to a complete refinishing job. The final tone of a stain cannot be predicted accurately. Matches can be attained only by trial and error. If the worn area is only a part of one surface, you may consider refinishing just that entire surface rather than the whole piece.

The proper procedure in match-staining is to mix some stain that looks as though it may be right and try it. You cannot make the trial on scrap wood since the wood affects the final color also. Try the stain on an inconspicuous part of the piece. Likely places are bottom surfaces of tabletops, inner surfaces of chest sides, and interior drawer parts. Several trials will be required.

When the correct stain has been found, it is applied to the worn area. We recommend that you wipe the stain as soon as it is applied. This usually results in the area being too light, but it can be darkened gradually by additional applications. If you overshoot and get it too dark, you can lighten the area by immediately wiping it with a cloth moistened with paint thinner. Allow to dry after lightening before proceeding. Complete mixing and staining instructions are found in Chapter 8.

Repairing

If your earlier examination of the piece disclosed other damages, they should be repaired at this stage. Needed repair work may be basic (structural) or surface (cosmetic) or both. These are explained fully in Chapters 7 and 9.

Restoring the Finish

When the piece has been cleaned, stained, and repaired, you are ready (finally!) to restore the finish. We will discuss the usual procedures, then some exceptions and special cases.

First, you should identify the old finish. An oil finish is easy to spot, but the hard clear finishes are another matter. There are very few persons who can distinguish between shellac, varnish, and lacquer by sight and touch alone. Someday you may be one of them. In the meantime, there is a simple test by which you can separate these common finishes.

The "clear finish test" should be performed on an inconspicuous bit of the finish, such as the inside top of a table leg or the bottom edge of a drawer front. Moisten one spot with denatured alcohol and another with lacquer thinner. If the spot under the alcohol softens, the finish is shellac. If the spot under the lacquer thinner softens, the finish is lacquer. If neither spot is affected, the finish is varnish.

THE HARD CLEAR FINISHES

With the finish identified, you must prepare the surface for additional finishing by rubbing it with 4/0 steel wool. Do not attempt to dig into the existing finish (admittedly difficult to do with 4/0 steel wool). Your purpose is twofold: first, to provide a "tooth" to which the new finish will adhere more securely and, second, to smooth out the surface irregularities found on any piece.

The steel wool is followed by a damp cloth to remove every particle of dust and steel. If the surface is irregular (carvings, moldings, joints), you should use a vacuum cleaner. Now, as an extra margin of safety, clean the surface again with paint thinner. This not only makes sure of dust and steel particles but of old wax, too. If any wax should remain, it will prevent some finishes from drying properly.

With the surface prepared and completely dry, you are ready to touch up the old finish. It is advisable to touch up with the same material used in the original finish. The simplest touching up is done with a spray can of lacquer, shellac, or varnish.

Effective use of spray cans is a little tricky. Following a few simple rules and with a little practice, however, you will be able to do it quite creditably.

The surface to be sprayed should be horizontal, if this is possible. The spray head must be neither too close nor too far from the surface. The proper distance depends on the structure of the head. Read the label. The nozzle must be held in the same position all the way across the surface—not "fanned out" as you reach the edge. Spraying should be at an angle of about 45 degrees to the horizontal surface. Spraying is accomplished by "sweeping" from side to side, beginning with the *nearer* edge and working toward the far edge. The spray should begin *before* the "sweep" reaches the side of the surface and continue until it has swept completely off the opposite side.

If you are a beginning sprayer, read the rules and spray a couple of old boards. Examine the results, reread the rules, and try again. Such practice will be more effective if you use smooth boards and paint rather than a clear finish. Mistakes will be more apparent. Be especially careful of overspraying too thick a coat. Not only are several thin coats superior to one thick one, but runs are less likely to occur.

Restoring with spray finishes is especially good when only a portion of a surface is to be covered. It is much easier to feather an edge with spray than with a brush. The brush is much more likely to leave a lap-edge at the outer edge of the repair.

If you insist on using a brush, make sure it is absolutely clean (preferably new), and thin the finish before applying. A good consistency requires about one-third thinner to two-thirds finish—denatured alcohol with shellac, lacquer thinner with lacquer, and paint thinner with varnish. The thinned finish material will help you avoid unevenness and too heavy a coat.

When dry, the final touch-up coat should be rubbed down gently with 4/0 steel wool. In cases of touching up only a portion of a surface, it is often advisable to apply a final thin coat to the entire surface in order to help equalize its appearance.

At this stage in the restoring process you may wish to make a slight improvement in the original. When working on a chest or table we frequently give the top surface an overcoat of varnish. Few original finishes are varnish, and we prefer to add this coat of protection against water and alcohol spills. It may be put over shellac or lacquer and is not detectable.

This brings up a point of honesty. The three clear finishes—shellac, varnish, and lacquer—will adhere perfectly well to each other. Any one of the three may be used to repair a piece. Believing, however, that restoring means to *original* condition, we always repair with the original finish. We do this even when planning to overcoat with varnish. In an emergency or as a convenience, the home refinisher may use whichever is handy.

When the final coat has been allowed to dry thoroughly, it is rubbed lightly with 4/0 steel wool. Gloss may be diminished by rubbing with 3/0 steel wool until the desired sheen is reached. Always use steel wool *with* the grain of the wood on flat surfaces.

OIL FINISHES

The average refinisher is seldom called on to restore an oil finish. This is indeed fortunate, since truly restoring a linseed-oil finish is an arduous task. The piece is cleaned and repaired and the original oil process begun. We will not repeat the gruesome details here. The purist is referred to Chapter 11.

We suggest that the home refinisher faced with this task face also the fact that there are times when general rules should be broken. We avoid working with linseed-oil finishes whenever possible. The process is so lengthy and charges are necessarily so high that most customers are all too glad to authorize a short cut. Certainly, we are speaking here of a dried-up linseed-oil finish that is in need of *restoring,* not of a fairly good finish that needs only normal maintenance to bring it up to par.

All this adds up to the following procedure. Clean and repair the piece in the recommended manner. Then apply Minwax Antique Oil Finish per instructions in Chapter 11. The time and effort are much less and the result is beautiful. Only a knowledgeable eye will distinguish this from a linseed-oil finish.

THE WAX FINISH

A so-called wax finish is by far the easiest to restore. The piece is simply cleaned, repaired, and waxed. Dressing (waxing) instructions are given in Chapter 12.

The opaque or paint finishes are the most difficult for the home refinisher to restore. Of course, some types are less of a problem than others.

The first task is to determine whether or not the paint is the *original* with which the piece was painted. A *re*painted piece is of no interest. A paint added five, twenty-five, or even fifty years ago is not worth the trouble of restoring. The basic problem in such cases is that the overcoats of newer paint cannot be removed while the original remains intact. The old comes off with the new. The piece must be refinished.

There is one significant exception to this situation. If you ever discover a bottom layer of paint that remains untouched by remover, you have found milk paint. Usually milk paint is worth restoring if it even approaches decent condition. The piece is cleaned and repaired. A matching mixture of milk paint is prepared and brushed on as needed. Of course, it may be sprayed with better results if a *good* sprayer is available. Detailed information on milk paint will be found in Chapter 10.

We suggest that you not attempt to use regular enamel in your restorations. Instead use "refinisher's enamel" to restore an enamel finish. Chapter 10 contains instructions for this special finish that can be worked to achieve perfect results. Even this, however, does not eliminate the lap-edge difficulty.

PAINTED DECORATIONS

Occasionally in the course of time you may be faced with restoring painted decorations on a piece. Good results can be achieved with patience. Basically, we use refinisher's enamel.

Decorative painting may be done with any convenient material— artist's oils, enamel, or even tempera or show-card paints. Our preference is flat interior paint. Whatever the medium, you must mix the colors to a careful match. Use small brushes appropriate in size and stiffness to the delicacy of the decoration. When complete and dry, cover the restored decoration with a thin coat of shellac. A further protective finish of shellac or varnish should be applied.

Dressing and Maintaining

Restored finishes must be dressed (waxed) and maintained in the same manner as any applied finishes. Dressing adds beauty and a measure of protection to a finish, while proper maintenance keeps it that way. Directions for these essential processes are found in Chapter 12. Note that oil finishes are *not* dressed.

French Polishing

There is a little-known but effective procedure for applying a finish that works quite well for touching-up and overcoating. It can even be used on a newly stained piece, but it is most useful in repairing old finishes. French polishing, as it is called, produces a very smooth coat of shellac that renews a worn finish—even filling and hiding minor scratches and thin spots. The result is a very high-gloss finish that can, however, be toned down with steel wool.

French polishing does require some skill. It is advisable for the beginner to practice before tackling a special project. Happily, though, if you make a mistake, correction without damage to the piece is easy.

Preparation for French polishing is standard for all restoring: thorough cleaning and repairing. In French polishing the shellac finish is applied with a cotton pad instead of a brush or sprayer. The applicator pad is made from a piece of old cotton sheet or shirt. Its shape is more like a ball than a pad so that you can grasp it firmly.

Wet the pad thoroughly with *boiled* linseed oil and squeeze out the excess. Put about a teaspoonful of shellac on the working surface of the pad. *Briskly* rub the pad on the area to be finished. The result is an unbelievably smooth coat of shellac.

French polishing is not as easy as it sounds. You will have two problems at first. Shellac and oil must be added to the pad as the work progresses. The proper amounts and proportion can be learned only by experience. Too much oil, and no shellac is deposited on the piece. Not enough oil, and too much shellac is deposited.

The second problem occurs when the pad sticks to the work

surface. This results in the impression of the cloth weave being left in the shellac. You can prevent this difficulty by two things. First, the pad must not stop moving when it is in contact with the piece. Keep it moving. If it does stop, it will stick to the shellac and leave an impression. Use a constant circular or figure-eight motion, beginning before the pad contacts the surface and continuing until you have lifted it clear. Second, a good deal of pressure must be applied to the pad. You must rub *hard* in order to force the shellac into the surface of the old finish. This pressure also helps to spread the shellac and produces heat from friction that dries it.

You can see that all this requires some practice—right combination of shellac and oil on the pad, hard pressure, and constant motion. Even several hours of practice will be amply repaid. Unless you give up working with furniture entirely, you will find your skill in French polishing useful time and again.

When you start your first French-polishing project you can count on both problems arising: shellac building up too rapidly and pad getting stuck. Do not be discouraged; this happens to everyone—even to the professional occasionally. Fortunately, they are easy to correct. Just moisten another pad with denatured alcohol and rub it over the problem area. Since alcohol is a solvent for shellac, the pad will pick it up. Use the alcohol pad until the problem is cleared, and start French polishing right away again.

French polishing is an amazing technique when first seen. It is ideal for a quick repair job. Skillfully applied and lightly steel-wooled (3/0) until its gloss matches the rest of the piece, a French-polish touch-up is difficult to detect.

Restoring the "Crazy Quilt"

Occasionally the refinisher encounters an old finish that looks like a crazy quilt. The entire finish is laced with cracks. In fact, it looks like a jigsaw puzzle with all the pieces pulled apart. This condition was caused by excessive temperatures and drying out. Although it looks hopeless, this finish often can be corrected with a little effort and patience.

Your first task is to identify the finish: shellac, varnish, or lacquer. This can be done with the test discussed earlier in this chapter. If the finish happens to be varnish, you are out of luck; it cannot be restored, so you must strip and refinish. Since there is so little varnish around, however, your bad finish is probably shellac or lacquer.

The restoration treatment for shellac and lacquer is the same except that the appropriate solvent is used: denatured alcohol for shellac and lacquer thinner for lacquer. The idea is to redissolve the finish, smooth it out, and let it dry. First, of course, you must carry out the standard cleaning and repairing procedures.

The treatment procedure is to brush the proper solvent on a section of the piece that has been turned horizontal if possible. Brush the solvent across the grain until the finish is dissolved. This happens very quickly. Then brush the liquefied finish lightly with the grain just as you would when applying a new finish. Do this to each section of the piece in turn and allow it to dry.

That is all there is to the procedure. In most cases the restored finish is quite thin. We recommend that an additional coat be applied. Of course, the new finish is steel-wooled and dressed as usual.

You may encounter a special situation with a shellac or lacquer finish. On occasion one of the ancients would mix a stain or color with the finish and apply them both at the same time. (This is analogous to the modern varnish-stain, which we do not recommend.) If you find this condition, it is all but impossible to smooth out the color evenly in the dissolved finish. Your best bet is to strip and refinish.

Restoring the "White Cloud"

We will mention one final special problem that the restorer may face. This is the finish that has white spots or clouds. Sometimes the entire finish may have an over-all whitish, cloudy appearance. This problem is caused by moisture, and you may be sure that the finish is shellac or lacquer, since moisture does not affect varnish.

Both shellac and lacquer will turn white if water is allowed to stand on them. Damp articles—glasses, flower pots, cloths—cause white spots down *in* the finish. Storage in a damp location can cause the entire piece to display this whitish condition. Fortunately, neither spots nor general cloudiness usually penetrate deeply into the finish. In these cases it can be removed by abrasion.

After cleaning, rub the affected area with 4/0 steel wool moistened in paint thinner. Examine the area frequently so that you can stop as soon as the discoloration is removed and not abrade more of the finish than necessary. The finish that remains after this procedure may be quite thin, so we recommend the application of an overcoat. If varnish is used for the overcoat, the area will be moistureproof.

Should the white spots extend throughout the depth of the finish, they may be removed by using the appropriate solvent. A moistened cloth (denatured alcohol for shellac or lacquer thinner for lacquer) is rubbed lightly over the area. This may lift all the finish, but it will not harm the wood beneath. If the water penetrated the finish, there will be dark spots in the wood. Your only recourse is to strip, bleach, and refinish.

Conclusion

The beginning refinisher is often surprised to learn that so many types of finish damage can be restored. Skillful restoration can be quite as satisfactory as complete refinishing. There is no doubt that it requires much less time and effort. The beginner should not jump right in with a can of remover until he has considered fully the potential of restoring.

Notes on New Furniture Finishes

Several times earlier we have made comments about the finishes found on new furniture. In nearly all cases it is simply one or two or a half-dozen coats of lacquer. Only on custom-made pieces are you likely to find shellac or varnish. By now you are well aware of the shortcomings of a lacquer finish—whether one coat or a dozen. In addition, most new furniture will be unfinished underneath and inside, and you know the disadvantages of that. Here, at the end of the processing chapters, we want to tell you what we do with all new furniture in order to make it serviceable.

First, we examine the piece thoroughly—inside, outside, and bottomsides. Any needed surface repairs are noted (often these are required, especially if the piece has been on a showroom floor).

Unfinished inner surfaces are checked, too.

The second step consists of giving the piece a *thorough* cleaning with paint thinner. Of course, this in no way harms the finish. It does remove dirt, dust, and any wax or polish that may have gotten on the piece in the store. In those rare instances when there is evidence that the piece has actually been waxed, we give the piece a *second* paint-thinner wash. Then we are sure that no wax remains to interfere with the new finish.

Next, every finished surface is rubbed lightly with 4/0 steel wool. This gives the factory finish a slight roughness to which our new finish will adhere better. The dust and steel-wool particles must be cleaned away carefully.

For long-time protection against moisture and drying, we next apply sealer/stain to *every* unfinished surface. This includes the inner and outer surfaces of the back, the bottom of the top, the inner sides, top and bottom of each dust board, and the inside and outside of every drawer. Matching the stain carefully is not necessary. These surfaces are normally out of sight, so if the color is in the right ball park, it is all right.

While the sealer/stain is drying on the inside, any needed surface repairs are made. Though damage is not unusual, it is often quite minor.

The new finish of varnish is applied after the sealer/stain has dried or after repairs are made. We put this protective varnish coat on every surface we can reach—inside and outside. If the piece is one that may suffer water or alcohol spills, we play it doubly safe and apply a second coat of varnish to the top surface.

The last step is to give the piece a good paste-wax dressing. Now it is ready for use and even a reasonable amount of misuse!

If you are not sure how to carry out any of the procedures in these steps, refer to the appropriate earlier chapters.

One further note about new furniture: Since you must correct the deficiencies in commercial finishes anyway, you need not be too concerned about the cosmetic condition of your purchases. If you want new furniture instead of old (we couldn't guess why), you can get it at a saving. Take advantage of "scratch and dent" sales, furniture outlet stores, and discontinued stock sales. You can easily fix up these pieces "like new."

III

Furniture—Knowing It and Getting It

14

Acquiring Furniture

Most home refinishers begin on furniture they have owned for some time. It may be a piece used daily or it may come from the attic or storeroom. Usually it is not something purchased "to refinish." Even so, the amateur refinisher soon develops the desire to acquire more pieces. This is a desire both to own more and to have more to refinish.

Acquiring furniture can be a great adventure. It can be as much or more fun than refinishing and using a piece. You may make a delightful "find" in storeroom or junk shop. You may get a great bargain—a "steal." You may know the joy of lengthy detective work and the success of locating a specific piece.

Acquiring furniture can be a great disaster also. You can get stuck and pay several times what a piece is worth. You may never "find" anything of special value or interest. The outcome is up to you.

We cannot give you good judgment. We can only give you a base of facts and knowledge from which you can exercise your own good judgment. We can suggest where to look, what to look for, and how to behave while you are there.

What to look for—not what pieces to look for but what to look for in the pieces that interest you—is the most important information you can have in this *game* of acquiring furniture. When you have studied the first two parts of this book and refinished one or two pieces, you will have a great deal of this knowledge. You will know something about the wood and about the quality of construction of any piece in which you are interested. You will be able to predict the ease or difficulty of repairing and refinishing. You will be able to judge the quality of any repairing and refinishing that has been done.

Add to this knowledge the information in the following chapters on authenticity and fakery and you will be in an excellent position to protect yourself and your purse. Most antique dealers are amazingly uninformed. When you know more than the dealer does, you are in the superior position.

Two related areas are important but beyond the scope of this book. You should become acquainted with the basics of furniture design. You need not become an expert, but you should learn the major characteristics of Queen Anne, for example, and how it differs from, say, Chippendale. Your local library and your local bookstore probably have a number of volumes containing this type of information.

The second kind of information you must get without our assistance is monetary. After examining a piece you should be able to place a fairly accurate dollar value on it. A printed table of values or prices is all but worthless. It cannot adequately describe condition. It is outdated when it comes off the press. In addition, prices vary greatly from one section of the country to another and from one type of piece to another.

In the final analysis, monetary value—like beauty—is in the eye of the beholder. The fair price depends on how badly one individual wants to sell and how badly another individual wants to buy. Nevertheless, in order to keep from getting stuck every time, you should have some knowledge of general market value. This can be acquired only by sampling the market. You should visit large and small shops and auctions periodically in order to determine asking prices in your area.

Earlier we referred to acquiring furniture as a "game." So it is for knowledgeable amateurs. It is a game between you and the dealer. You will be surprised to discover that it is a game for most dealers as well—more serious, perhaps, but still a game. Most small and many large dealers are in the business because they like furniture and other people who like it. They enjoy bantering and arguing about finishes, refinishing, construction, and value. The more you know, the more you can enjoy and profit from this game. It is completely different from the experience of acquiring new furniture.

One further general point should be made. There are *no* rules for what pieces will go together in a room. From the standpoint of period and style, a very wide range is considered compatible today. Unless two pieces are to stand side by side, almost any two can be placed in the same room. If it is pleasing to you, it will be pleasing to others. The kind of wood and the type of finish are of even less importance. When you see a good piece at a good price and you want it, buy it. It will fit in.

Old Furniture and Antiques

In our business we make a distinction between used furniture, old furniture, and antiques. The lines between them are not hard and clear. In fact the only sure thing is that none of the three categories includes new furniture.

Legally, an antique is a piece that is more than 100 years old. In practice an antique is considered anything that has acquired unusual value due to its beauty and scarcity and because of its age—often as little as fifty years.

We call used furniture anything that is not new and has no value due to age or special characteristics. Used furniture is practically valueless under normal circumstances. If you do not believe this, try to sell something to a dealer in used furniture. It may be useful, but it is not valuable.

Old furniture falls between the two. It is better than used furniture but not as good as an antique. Old furniture will be antique some day, but it isn't yet worthy enough.

More often than not the tags "old" and "antique" are used interchangeably. We frequently use the word *old* to include antique.

You can see that there are great gray areas between these categories. As they are used, the definitions are nebulous. There is a saying in the trade: "One person's antique is another's junk." That's the way it is.

Follow the signs along the highways and byways to the advertised "Antiques" and you will find few true antiques. Most of their offerings will be "old," with a scattering of "used." Some of them will have mostly or even entirely used pieces.

You should get what you like and what you want without too much care about its classification. Just watch what you pay. Be careful of the fellow (or the little old lady) who caresses a table from the 1930s and solemnly swears that it was in a neighbor's family for at least 150 years. You should be able to spot this. Then regard everything else he says in the game as a probable exaggeration—or lie, if you prefer!

Noncommercial Sources of Furniture

You should not overlook noncommercial sources of good pieces. The storerooms, attics, barns, and basements of this country are full of old furniture. Grandparents, parents, aunts, uncles, brothers, and sisters—nearly everyone has them. Among the good pieces there are the occasional outstanding pieces. If only you could get at them!

Now that you know how to refinish furniture, you are in a better position than most to make use of such stored pieces. It's not that they couldn't do it; they just hesitate and put it off indefinitely. As your reputation as a refinisher grows (and it surely will), conversation turns to old furniture with increasing frequency. This provides your opening, first to "see" a stored piece and later, perhaps, to acquire it.

Often such acquisitions are without cost. In such cases it is both polite and good groundwork for the next time to send your benefactor a small gift. Who can tell what he might offer as a result of such expressed appreciation!

Speaking of gifts, we advise that you never turn down a gift of old furniture. You may not really want the piece offered, but refusing the first may forestall a second or third later. Take it and store it—even dispose of it. You can always make an excuse for its not being displayed. "I haven't yet had time" or "The side splintered completely" or "It was crushed when Bob's pet elephant knocked it over."

Frequently you can acquire a desired piece by offering to refinish another stored piece for the owner in exchange. The barter of craftsmanship for goods is as old as civilization. It works as well today. In many situations it is the ideal solution. Since "filthy" money is never mentioned, neither party is embarrassed. This is also the case if you offer to trade a refinished piece that you have for one that you prefer.

Circumstances may favor purchasing from or "reimbursing" a relative for a stored piece. Let the situation and your conscience be your guide. Treat Aunt Hattie right and you will both come out ahead.

All that has been said about relative-pack rats applies equally to friends and neighbors. Everyone is looking for a good deal, and a deal can be good for both sides. This is true of gifts, trades, and reimbursements.

One of our early aquisitions was a beautiful old rolltop desk, which we still use today. We traded a beat-up mandolin to a neighbor, who was offered the desk by his Aunt Hattie. He was afraid to turn it down, and she never knew that we helped him move it not to his house but to ours. Wonder if he still has that mandolin and if it has given him one tenth the pleasure we have had from the desk? Probably each of us still thinks he came out ahead—that is, if the memory wasn't discarded years ago along with the mandolin.

As you become known as an "old furniture nut," opportunities will seek you out. Friends and acquaintances will make it a point to give you news. It usually begins, "You may be interested . . ." George Willoughby is disposing of an estate that includes some old furniture. The Johnsons are moving into an apartment and haven't space for half their stuff. The Greens are redecorating and throwing out their old dining-room furniture. Such leads can produce anything from junk to antiques.

Discards are another source that should not be overlooked. People often buy new furniture and simply throw out the old. As you learn more about old furniture, you will be amazed by what some people throw away. You may prefer not to check the city dump yourself periodically, but you can have it done. In smaller localities, especially, the fellow who operates the bulldozer will be glad to do that for you. If he has an idea of what you want, he will often hold likely pieces until you can check them. A few dollars now and then for his trouble can pay off handsomely.

Once we were asked to refinish an old chair. The customer was well known; she moved in the "right circles." It happened that we had seen that particular chair not too long before as it lay beside a curb awaiting the trash collector. We don't know how it was acquired by the customer, since we did not ask. Like so many pieces, this chair did not look like the same one when it left the shop. It would have graced any home.

Old furniture is where you find it. Good pieces become more scarce all the time. More people are trying to acquire them, and the prices rise accordingly. And antiques or even good old furniture are not being made any longer. Get it when and where you can. In your searching, remember: one fellow's junk is . . .

Commercial Sources of Furniture

In spite of the foregoing, most of us have to get much if not all of our old furniture from commercial sources. By far the most interesting and exciting source is the auction.

Auctions are not only fascinating to most people but they can be quite dangerous financially. You can attend an auction and get a bargain sometimes or lose your shirt anytime. This is a very specialized marketplace—so specialized and exciting that we have devoted an entire following chapter to it.

Antique shops come in all shapes and sizes. At times it seems as though they proliferate throughout the countryside like weeds. They are large and small, honest and crooked, and stocked with every class of merchandise. The byword in all of them is *caveat emptor* —let the buyer beware.

We do not mean to imply that all dealers in old and antique furniture are dishonest. Of course, some are out-and-out crooked. The chapter on fakery will help you spot these fellows. Most dealers, however, are reasonably honest at least. All dealers are in business to make money and charge what the traffic will bear. Even the scrupulously honest sometimes have a distorted opinion of what the traffic should bear. Even they will exaggerate statements of age or condition from time to time.

Only an extremely small number of dealers will offer any kind of a guarantee on their merchandise. A few of these will provide a written statement of the age and, perhaps, the lineage of a piece. For the most part, however, it is a matter of buy it and it is yours. Buying an old or antique piece is *not* like buying a coat and returning it because of a poorly sewn seam. *Caveat emptor.* Know the other fellow's merchandise.

Perhaps your greatest danger is the dealer who is ignorant—ignorant of furniture, of refinishing, of finishes. He will tell you anything and appear honest because he believes his own misstatements. If it sounds good and is in his favor, this dealer believes and repeats anything a supplier or a previous customer tells him. As your own knowledge increases and you visit more shops, you will be stunned at the number of dealers of this type that you find. They can only stay in business because there are a very large number of ignorant buyers around. *Caveat emptor.*

Understandably, we are most upset by one particular type of ignoramus. That is the dealer-refinisher who personally botches up his merchandise before selling it. It may be a man or a little old lady, but there are plenty of them around. They "refinish" without knowing anything about refinishing. Sometimes the sight of their products comes close to causing physical illness: a fine old walnut chest that had a repaired top—several tack holes had been drilled out and plugged with *one-inch dowels of pine;* a sturdy oak table that was subjected to a power sander until the points of a dozen screws shone brightly through the top.

Once we were examining an authentic hutch table, trying to determine how it had become mutilated, when the lady dealer-refinisher said proudly, "I had a terrible time getting that piece in shape. I had to plane the top forever before it was right. Would you believe that top was two inches thick when I got it?" Things are obviously worse than we said. Not only are old and antique pieces no longer being made, but they are being systematically mutilated and destroyed!

You will probably soon become interested only in unrefinished pieces. Of course, they are less expensive, but, more importantly, they have not been butchered by some so-called refinisher. With just a little study and experience you will be able to do a better job than 90 percent of the dealer-refinishers.

Since you buy from dealers on an "as is" basis, it is the custom that you be allowed to examine the merchandise as fully as you wish. By all means take advantage of this custom and examine every piece thoroughly, inside and out. We cannot say that all dealers who prohibit inspections are crooks, but we do advise you to walk out of such shops—fast. *Caveat emptor.*

The matter of bargaining over price is quite interesting. Some dealers absolutely refuse and some are "insulted" if you do not bargain. Most dealers peg the marked or asking price as high as they hope to get. They expect to bargain but, of course, are delighted if you do not and simply pay the asking price.

Neither size, honesty, nor sex makes a dealer a bargainer or a nonbargainer. You never know which is which unless you try. Whether or not they are willing, dealers expect the attempt. An honest nonbargaining dealer will not be upset in the least by your invitation to bargain. *Caveat emptor.*

It is you who will have to initiate the bargaining. Not until you start to leave empty-handed will the dealer invite bargaining. Even then most won't because you may return and pay the asking price. If you are inexperienced and hesitant about bargaining, jump in anyway; you won't learn this fine art any younger.

We can't turn you into a finished bargainer, for this is an art—frequently a subtle art. Often what is not said is more important than the words used. We can offer you some approaches to help you over your hesitancy and get you started. The variety of openings is unlimited.

Here are some comments that may get the bargaining started: This marked price is quite steep. This marked price is a good asking price, but you surely don't hope to get that much. What's your *asking* price for this piece? Oh, I couldn't possibly spend that much! That's over my budget for a piece like this. Why, I think more like XX dollars for this piece. It's not worth more than XX dollars to me. XX dollars is my final offer. Well, if you decide to price it more reasonably, let me know—I may still be interested.

This may sound quite strange to you, but that's the way it is done. You don't hear it in the dress or shoe shop, but it is frequently heard in most antique shops. Several pointers will help you as the bargaining proceeds.

First, attempt your bargaining out of earshot of other customers. The dealer may refuse if he thinks it may prevent another customer from paying asking prices. Secondly, decide what you are willing to pay early. In bringing his price down, the dealer may get you to pay more than you really think it's worth. You could get so excited with your success at bargaining that you still pay too much. Make your initial dollar offer lower than the price you are willing to pay. This allows you to come up while the dealer comes down and makes it possible for both of you to be "successful." Finally, don't expect to win every time you bargain. Life just *ain't* like that. Take a defeat in stride and in good spirit and try another day. Now, we ask you, doesn't this game become more fun all the time?

Search out dealers whenever you are away from your home area and have a little time to "explore." Now and then you will be surprised at what you find. Some years ago we happened on an excellent shop and dealer in the most unlikely place. This fellow was out in the country on a secondary road in a village of no more than seventy-five souls. The closest small town was ten miles away. He had a small sign in front of an old house close to the road, but that house was crowded with beautiful pieces—a few of museum quality. George did his own refinishing, and he was a skilled craftsman with a real appreciation for fine work. To top it all, his prices were quite reasonable. We visited him several times before lightning destroyed the house and all his fine furniture. He left that area, but one day we will find him again—refinishing furniture, no doubt!

You may be surprised at what you find if you get off the interstate highways. When taking a trip we usually pull a small utility trailer in case we are fortunate enough to discover a real bargain. Your chances of making a "find" are better in rural areas, but watch out for tourist traps.

You should not overlook the "junquetique" and plain junk shops in your area and in your travels. Often a shop labeled junquetique looks better on the inside than some so-called antique shops.

We will mention just one more commercial source of old furniture. Though it is quite obvious, most people overlook the used-furniture dealers. These fellows sometimes have good old pieces buried among the used stuff. Again, rural dealers are more likely prospects. You will have to find the store and the furniture, so take your flashlight and ask to rummage through his back room or storage shed. When you do find a piece, the price usually will be reasonable. Some of our most interesting, if not oldest, pieces came from used-furniture stores.

Funds for Acquiring Furniture

We have discussed much about buying old and antique furniture. Good pieces are often expensive, and prices rise faster than most incomes. Very few of us have unlimited or even sufficient funds to purchase all the furniture we would like. Aside from continuing to search for bargains, there are some ways to increase your purchasing power. If you are like most people, these opportunities will come to you.

As your refinishing skills improve, you will acquire a reputation among friends who have seen your work in your home. Invariably, the day will come when one of them will ask you to refinish a piece. Later there will be others and, then, friends of friends. Good refinishers are hard to find, and the word will get around.

You will have to decide whether or not you will refinish for others. If you do so, remember that friendship is friendship and business is business. Surely your friend who owns a clothing store does not provide you dresses free of cost. Neither should you provide refinishing services free of cost. Professional refinishers charge *plenty,* and you should charge enough to make your time and effort worthwhile. This can be a handy source of cash for your own purchases.

A couple of other sources of funds will become available to you. You would probably be surprised at the number of people in your community who want an old and well-refinished occasional table or chair. You may well have one or two extra pieces as you buy and refinish to replace something you are using. You may also purchase an extra table or chair when you discover special bargains (dealers will often give special prices when you buy several pieces). In most communities a small newspaper ad will bring a number of calls for your "extra" pieces. Profit from these sales can increase your buying power for pieces you want, or more extra pieces to sell.

In many communities you can allow your "business" to grow as much as you wish. You can keep it small and occasional, but often the demand for good work is so great that a full-time and very profitable business could develop.

Conclusion

There is a skill to acquiring old furniture whether it comes from attics or shops. Purchasing, especially, is fraught with dangers for the beginner. One does not buy it as one does new furniture. It's more like buying a used car.

In order to be successful you must know furniture and refinishing. You must know where to look for it and the "tricks of the trade" after you find it. This knowledge is available to you, and it is not difficult to acquire.

Acquire the knowledge and you can acquire the furniture at reasonable cost. You can even use your knowledge and skill to help finance your purchases.

15

Signs of Authenticity

It seems that the old and antique furniture business has more than its share of frauds and fradulent sales. Many of these frauds actually are plainly dishonest. They deliberately misrepresent the age and other characteristics of their merchandise. They will sell as antiques and at corresponding prices pieces they know to be fakes. Some of them even make these bogus pieces themselves. Unscrupulous dealers are clever and financially dangerous. Dishonest frauds, however, are greatly outnumbered by the ignorant frauds.

This business abounds with ignorant dealers. They are frauds not so much because they misrepresent their merchandise (though they do it) but because they misrepresent *themselves.* They can't tell an authentic piece from a bogus one, though it all but speaks to them. As a result, everything they have is genuine; everything is very old; everything is very valuable. They believe and pass on to the customer everything their suppliers tell them. They bilk the public of plenty.

In spite of the many honest and informed dealers, the picture is quite dismal. And whose fault is it? The fault is yours—you, the consumer. Dishonest frauds will always be with us, but the ignorant frauds can stay in business only because nearly all buyers of old pieces are *more* ignorant. They, too, believe what they are told.

Most people "shop" before they buy clothes, appliances, automobiles—everything but antiques. For some reason, when it comes to buying old furniture they won't read or study about it first. They won't compare merchandise and prices at different stores. They won't even examine the merchandise closely or carefully. No wonder there are many frauds in the business!

At least you can protect yourself. This chapter and the one that follows will provide you with basic information to detect misrepresentations. Of course, only considerable study and experience can make you an *expert*. This is only the beginning, but it is enough that you should be able to spot the ignorant dealers (they give themselves away in so many ways). At best, the dishonest will be able to sell you only the really good fakes!

In this chapter we will discuss finishes and construction details as they are related to age and wear and, simply, the passage of time. The following chapter contains discussions of deliberate misrepresentations.

Examiner's Tool Kit

The only way you can protect yourself in the old-furniture marketplace is to examine the merchandise *thoroughly*. Cursory examination of a piece, even when coupled with extensive knowledge of what to look for, can be very misleading. Certainly, the more money involved, the more thorough the examination must be.

As mentioned earlier, no legitimate dealer will object to inspection of his wares. Of course, it is your responsibility to see that your examination does not damage the piece under consideration. The dealer who forbids such an inspection probably has something to hide.

Every potential buyer should carry his own examining kit. It is unreasonable to expect the dealer to furnish you with tools. One item is absolutely essential to perform an adequate inspection. Only a good bright flashlight will enable you to see clearly the undersides and insides of furniture. The recesses in a piece will usually tell you more than the outside about its age—but only if you can see in there. Our kit contains a *good* pencil-type flashlight. We keep a larger, stronger flashlight in the car in case the one in the kit should not be adequate.

Our kit is small so that we can carry it everywhere. Thus, it can include only the basics. In addition to the light, there are only two other items. One is a small steel tape measure for detecting warping, wood shrinkage, and for determining other potentially changed dimensions.

The last examining-kit item is a scout-type knife. The blade is useful for scraping in hidden places to look for older layers of finish below the top one and to get a glimpse at the wood under opaque finishes. The screwdriver blades—one regular, one Phillips—are used to get a look at screws and to get further inside some pieces. (The bottle opener may be very useful on a long, dry day!)

Obviously, our "kit" will fit into a pocket or purse. Any dealer would get nervous if you walked in carrying a toolbox. The kit tools are almost always sufficient. In case the dealing gets serious and a large piece is involved, other tools are as close as the car outside. In addition to the larger flashlight there are several sizes of calipers; small containers of denatured alcohol, lacquer thinner, Kwik, and ammonia; and assorted small tools.

At the very least, carry a light when shopping. Without it, you are buying the proverbial pig in a poke.

Finishes and Age

At the outset, let us caution you that no one sign makes a piece authentic any more than one tree makes a forest. One road sign will not get you from New York to California, and one sign of authenticity will not get you from the bogus to the genuine. In traveling cross-country, the greater the distance, the more signs you will need. In antiquing, the greater the value and age, the more signs you should require.

The type and condition of a finish can sometimes serve as a good general indication of age. The first problem is to determine whether the finish is the original one or one that has replaced the original. If a piece has been refinished, it is obvious that the amount of time between construction of the piece and application of the present finish cannot be determined.

A relatively recent refinishing job on an old piece causes you to think that only extraordinary circumstances could have preserved a finish so well for so long. Then, too, it is a very rare thing for any refinisher to remove all traces of the original finish. Such traces are seldom on the outside, but an examination of hidden surfaces will frequently reveal them. The bottom sides of tops, the upper and inner surfaces of legs, and the bottom edges of drawer fronts and any vertical parts are good places to examine.

If you are convinced that you are dealing with an original finish, several factors are related to age. A paint finish places the question squarely on your judgment since paint itself tells you little. You just have to judge how old and chipped and worn it appears to be in relation to the claimed age and probable use of the piece. Even milk paint doesn't authenticate age, since it can be mixed easily in kitchen or shop today.

The hard clear finishes, on the other hand, may tell you a great deal about the age of a piece. More correctly, they may tell you how old a piece is *not*. These finishes are shellac, varnish, and lacquer. All three are in use today, but they were developed at different times.

Lacquer was developed in the early part of this century, but it received little use until around the time of World War I. At that time the special qualities of lacquer, particularly its very fast drying time, were recognized as being ideally suited to the production line. Since then, practically all mass-produced furniture has been given a lacquer finish. At any rate, an original lacquer finish indicates that a piece does not predate 1900 and probably does not predate World War I.

Varnish was developed first about 1850, but for many years it was used only on a regional basis. In fact, varnish has never been widely used in spite of its several superior qualities. This finish is and has been used by the quality cabinet and furniture maker and by the quality refinisher almost exclusively. As to age, a piece with an original varnish finish is no earlier than 1850.

The remaining clear hard finish is shellac. This is the oldest of these

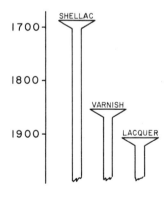

AGE AND FINISH

finishes. Shellac was in use before 1700.

With practice the beginner can learn to distinguish fairly well between shellac, varnish, and lacquer. Appearance and resistance to knife or fingernail pressure will usually tell the story. (See Chapter 11 for the characteristics of each.) In the meantime, there is the simple test described earlier. Shellac is dissolved by denatured alcohol, lacquer by lacquer thinner, and varnish by neither.

Construction Details and Age

The most reliable signs of authenticity are found in the methods of construction used on a piece. Both the elements of design and the mechanics of woodworking are significant. We shall not discuss design here, since countless volumes have been written on the subject. You are urged to visit a bookstore or library and to become familiar with the basics. Suffice it to say here that you must know enough to prevent your getting caught paying a fancy price for a piece that is obviously Early Victorian because the seller tells you that it was made "about 1700."

There are a number of things to look for in the mechanics of construction of a piece. One of these is the marks made by the tools used in construction. In commercial furniture, as opposed to home-made pieces, tool marks faded out about 1850 with the development of modern, fast power tools. Prior to that time, even power tools were crude and slow, and they left their marks on the unfinished (and sometimes the finished) surfaces of the wood.

Before 1850 only the exposed wood surfaces received more than a rough smoothing. It was too laborious before the appearance of the fast-turning joiner. The back boards, the inner surfaces of case pieces, the back parts of drawers, and other such parts were left rough. Long after this date most pieces had some rough surfaces. The marks made by hand plane, chisel, and saw are often visible on such surfaces.

Rotary power saws slowly replaced reciprocal power saws about 1850. Thus, curved saw marks first began to appear about that date. Prior to that, saw marks were straight. The reciprocal saws (early 1700s to about 1850) left marks that are straight and perpendicular to the edge of the wood. Straight marks that are slanted (not 90

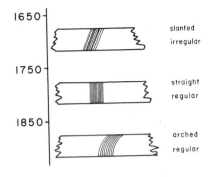

1650 — slanted irregular

1750 — straight regular

1850 — arched regular

AGE AND SAW MARKS

degrees to the edge) and that lack uniformity were made by hand from the 1600s to the present.

The year 1850 also marks the dividing line between slow lathes and modern fast ones. The old lathes often left tool marks on turned parts. These parts also tended to be rather irregular, since matching of dimensions was often done by eye.

The nails in a piece can be a very helpful indication of age. Modern, machine-made nails date from about 1875. Cut nails were first made around 1800. Prior to 1800 all nails were hand-forged. These were generally square in cross-section and tapering to a point. Fortunately, it is not necessary to pull out a nail to determine its type. Hand-made nails have heads that are rough, slightly to considerably domed, and usually square though sometimes nearly round. Cut nails have rectangular heads that were smooth and flat after about 1825.

The first screws were hand-made around 1600 by laboriously hand-filing threads on a piece of rod and sawing a slot in the top. They were untapered—straight and blunt. In the early 1800s crude machine-made screws appeared. These were slightly tapered but still blunt with slots that had been sawed. The modern, sharp-pointed screw was introduced about 1850—that magic year.

Wooden pegs are often found in old furniture. Of course, they were used before metal fasteners (nails and screws) were made. However, they were often used instead of metal fasteners for more solid and long-lasting construction. The mere presence of wooden pegs is *not* an indication of great age.

Dovetail joints can be helpful in dating a piece. This type of joint

Signs of Authenticity   155

is found most frequently at the front corners of drawers. The dove-tailing parts of these joints were large and irregular prior to the middle of the last century. Then, machine-made dovetail joints appeared, and the parts became progressively smaller and more regular.

Perhaps it is well to pause here a moment and point out the obvious by reminding you that a development or invention cannot be used before it is discovered. For example, sharp-pointed ma-chine-made wood screws could not have been used before 1850. The converse is *not* true. Hand-made screws and hand-made dove-tail joints *can* appear in and on a piece made yesterday. The trick in this authenticating game is to find the newest original characteristic of a piece and that gives you the earliest date of construction.

There are a few other construction factors that should be men-tioned even though no very firm dates can be attached to them. Modern drawer bottoms, for example, are of uniform thickness. Old drawer bottoms are quite thick, with just the edges shaved down thin

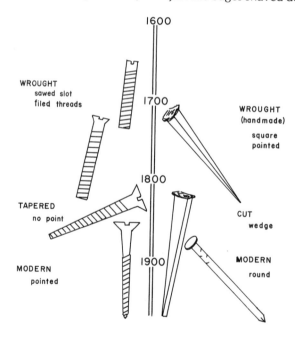

SCREWS   AND   AGE   AND   NAILS

enough to fit into the front and side slots. Logic would indicate that this development corresponds to the change-over from reciprocal to rotary saws.

Early moldings were usually simple and large. They are almost always uneven. Interestingly, before the mid-1800s they were fastened with small nails or pegs rather than glue.

Hardware, other than that already mentioned, can provide some guidance. The difficulty, of course, is that knobs and pulls are so easily changed and that so many old designs are being made today for legitimate reproductions. One should attempt to determine if the hardware is original. The match between the design period of a piece and the design of the hardware is the first clue. Evidence of extra

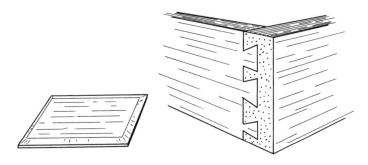

1850

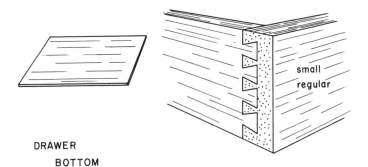

DRAWER
BOTTOM

LAP DOVETAIL JOINT

and/or misplaced holes is another indication of replacement hardware, as are signs of wear on the wood itself. Often this wear does not correspond to the location or design of the present knobs or pulls. Old hardware was usually fastened with bolts that passed from the front with a nut (often roughly made) on the inside. Modern and reproduction hardware frequently has the bolt installed from the inside to the outside where it screws into the knob or pull.

A reliable indication of the age of wood is the shrinkage that has taken place since the piece of furniture was constructed. As wood ages it shrinks in one dimension but not another. Drying out over the years causes wood to contract *across* the grain, often to an obvious extent. Along the direction of the grain the amount of shrinkage is so extremely small that, for all practical purposes, it can be ignored. Unfortunately, the rate of shrinkage across the grain is not constant. The amount of change depends on the type of wood, the type of finish used, and the humidity and temperature to which it was subjected over the years. So even though we cannot say, for example, that a board loses 2 percent of its width every thirty years, we can get some valuable clues from the fact that wood does contract across the grain.

One of the easiest places to become acquainted with shrinkage is in the bottoms of drawers of such pieces as chests, dressers, desks, and cabinets. Drawer bottoms usually show the most marked change in dimensions because they are thin wood and, in American furniture, they were almost always made of soft wood and almost never had a finish applied to them. Drawer bottoms usually fit into grooves in the front and side pieces and are fastened with a small nail or brad to the bottom of the back piece. Further, except in narrow, deep drawers, the grain direction is from side to side. Consequently, the bottom board shrinks from front to back. Since the back is attached, the front edge pulls right out of the slot. In extreme cases there may be a gap of three quarters of an inch or more between the bottom and the drawer front.

Evidence of shrinkage can be found in round tabletops. Careful measurement will show that such a piece is narrower across the grain than with the grain. The slightly oval shape is a good indication of age.

Shrinkage in a piece constructed with pegs causes a condition that is mistakenly regarded as a problem but which is, in reality, good

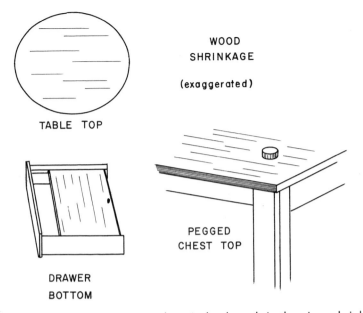

TABLE TOP

WOOD
SHRINKAGE

(exaggerated)

DRAWER
BOTTOM

PEGGED
CHEST TOP

evidence. The important point here is that boards in the piece shrink and leave the peg projecting slightly above the surface because its grain direction is from end to end. Running one's fingers lightly over the top of a chest of peg construction will reveal the protruding pegs. Of course, this condition does not prevail in a newly constructed piece or in an old piece that some fool has sanded.

In our discussion of the signs of authenticity we now come to a topic that is difficult to describe. It cannot, even, be shown in a photograph. You must actually experience patina in order to understand it, for patina is a mental impression created by the surface appearance of old furniture. A piece that receives any use at all will acquire over the years innumerable minute dents and scratches that are individually imperceptible. These, coupled with subtle changes that occur in wood when it has long exposure to light, create the effect called patina. The look of such a piece has been called velvety, mellow, softened, deep, and rich. Beside such a beautiful surface, modern pieces look harsh. In order to be able to appreciate fully and judge patina, you should study old furniture in museums, in the better antique shops, and in the homes of your friends. You will soon acquire a feeling for it.

Of all the signs of authenticity, this intangible called patina is probably the most reliable, for we know of no way to create it artificially, though we have seen a few special finishes that imitate it rather well. Patina does indicate age, but, most unfortunately, the lack of patina is not a sure sign of a lack of age. We are most distressed that amateur home refinishers and so-called professional refinishers in increasing numbers appear to be resorting to the use of sandpaper and power sanders in their work. From what you now know about patina, you can realize that sanding the surface of a board "to make it smooth" removes the patina before it removes anything else. This is why authentic but patina-less antiques are found in shops and homes.

In checking the authenticity of old pieces you must become sensitive to signs of wear from normal use. Case pieces with drawers will have runners and drawer sides that are worn from countless openings and closings, often so bad that the drawers no longer fit well. Kitchen and dining tables will show more wear in those areas of the top where you would expect people to be sitting. Rocking-chair rockers will be worn considerably more in the center than near the ends. Any piece with foot rests or pedals, such as an organ or piano, will show considerable wear, even on metal. Chair rungs, though not made for feet, will have evidence of their having been present.

The feet and legs of all kinds of furniture will display the scuff marks of vacuum cleaners, mops, shoes, and the like. Many pieces with wooden feet will even be worn on the bottom from having been moved about.

The long and short of wear is that no furniture was made and placed in a glass case. Even parlor furniture was used occasionally and cleaned around. All pieces will show some signs of wear appropriate to their intended function and subsequent use.

Conclusions

In this chapter you have learned how a number of factors can be used to authenticate the age of a piece—finishes, gross and detailed aspects of construction, aging of wood, and wear from normal use. All of these characteristics are reliable *provided* there are no crooks in the deal. Every one of them, however, can be successfully simulated today. Every one of them has been and is being simulated. There are a lot of recently constructed "antiques" on the market *and* in homes.

You can protect yourself from the dishonest frauds and the ignorant frauds only by applying your knowledge in thorough inspections. Even then you will be duped now and then. Even the experts get fooled occasionally. It happens to everyone. They just don't know about it or, if they do, they don't boast about it.

You can only reduce the chances that you will be "taken." Information in the next chapter on fakes will help you do this.

16

Signs of Fakery

There is a flourishing business today in manufacturing bogus antique furniture. Unscrupulous operators are attracted because of increasingly higher prices and because of the woeful ignorance of the typical buyer of old furniture. Many bogus pieces are well executed and difficult to detect. Most, however, are poorly done—just good enough to fool the typical buyer. The reason is that really good fakes are expensive to *make!*

We stated earlier that all the signs of authenticity can be imitated. Fortunately, most of them can be imitated only by hand; machines can do the job only well enough to fool the very ignorant. Hand labor is the most expensive part of any manufacturing process today. Consequently, the manufacturer of fakes faces a dilemma: He can sink most of his potential profit into the job or he can settle for imitating just two or three signs of authenticity.

If the fake is of a rare piece that is expected to bring a very high price, the manufacturer will go to great lengths. In all but the most rare, however, he depends on the customer's ignorance or carelessness to enable him to get by with a few signs. He trusts that the examination, if there is one, will not go beyond the signs he provides. At least nine times out of ten he is right—and safe. On that rare occasion when his fake is discovered, he woefully exclaims that he was certainly taken in by the little gray-haired lady who sold it to him!

We will tell you some of the things to search for (and hope that you do not find) while you are looking for the signs of authenticity. The main point is to look beyond the obvious characteristics of the piece. Only in the most expensive pieces is it worthwhile for the faker to take care of all the details. You can catch him on the less expensive ones, and you should employ an expert for the others. We should point out that the expert should be someone *other* than the dealer from whom you are buying.

No legitimate dealer will object to a close examination of his merchandise by you or anyone you may bring in. As we have said, everyone makes mistakes, especially in authenticating antiques. If you discover a fake in an honest shop, they will be upset—not because you discovered it but because they were cheated and almost cheated someone else. Especially, you will not find the same piece for sale when you go back later.

You will notice that we have used the words *fake* and *misrepresentation* but not *reproduction*. The reason for this is that a reproduction is a legitimate copy of an old piece. It is deliberately constructed to appear superficially authentic. It is not made or sold to deceive. Dishonesty enters the picture only if it is offered for sale as an original (and even though it may have had a little artful doctoring, it is fairly easy to detect).

There is nothing wrong with selling or buying a reproduction—at a reproduction price. Some pieces of furniture are simply unavailable in the original. Others are prohibitively expensive. After all, there were only so many William and Mary highboys made. A reproduction may be desired to round out a collection that would otherwise remain incomplete, or because it is an attractive, useful piece. If so, buy it with no misgivings or apologies.

There is, of course, another kind of so-called reproduction and that is one made of antique wood for the definite purpose of deceiving. There is a flourishing business in lumber from old, old houses, and a good deal of it finds its way into cabinets, tables, chests, and the like that are offered (and bought) as antiques. In addition to the signs already discussed, there are a couple of special things to watch out for here.

An examination of the inside, unfinished surfaces will frequently reveal unused nail holes. They may be sitting there in all their glory or an attempt may have been made to fill and hide them. There may be paint or traces of paint on one board and not on an adjoining one. More subtly, there may be faded and nonfaded areas on an individual board where part of it was protected over the years. Such anomalies cannot be explained away.

Another type of misrepresentation is the conversion of an authentic antique into one that is more rare and valuable. A saw and a sander are all a crook needs to convert a plain cupboard into a Welch dresser or common cottage furniture into Early American. Empire pieces, which are usually pine with mahogany veneer, are changed into Early American by soaking off the veneer. Flat-top highboys are divided into a lowboy and chest. Rockers are converted into straight chairs by removing the rockers and splicing the legs to lengthen them. Straight chairs become rockers. The list is endless, and your only protection is close examination and thorough familiarity with styles. For example, former cottage pieces have regular, machine-made dovetail joints, and the sides of the case pieces are paneled instead of solid. Former Empire pieces still look like Empire with their heavy framing, boxy lines, and overhanging tops.

While there is no excuse—except dishonesty, of course—for the types of conversions mentioned, there is a reason for this next category of misrepresentations. The excuse is for *making* some of them but *not* for misrepresenting them. Often, true antiques are partially damaged beyond repair. In other cases parts are lost. When authentic parts are assembled to create one piece of furniture, the result is usually called a marriage. This seems to happen with tables more frequently than with other pieces. For example, the remaining top of one Sheraton table and the remaining pedestal of another may be assembled to form a true Sheraton table. While neither was of use alone, the marriage produced a usable and true, but not original, Sheraton. The piece is even valuable, though not as valuable as an original in equal condition.

Other kinds of marriages involve the feet of chests, desks, and so on. Drop leaves on tables also may not be original. Occasionally a table may be so badly damaged on the edges that they are simply cut off and the top becomes a bit smaller.

Your only protection from this form of misrepresentation is, again, close inspection. The discerning eye can sometimes detect a discrepancy where the parts are attached or a subtle lack of proper proportion. A very good marriage is hard to find.

Similar to marriages are instances of replacements. In this case, broken or missing parts are made from new wood or even from old wood. New feet, legs, leaves, tops, and doors may be added. A neat trick on a valuable piece is to replace a damaged drawer front—not the whole front, just the outside quarter inch or so. Obviously, the wood grain is different on the two sides of what is supposed to be a solid board. A replacement can save an otherwise useless piece. The value, however, is reduced according to the nature and extent of the replacement part or parts. Watch for previously discussed signs and especially signs of modern workmanship.

The final type of misrepresentation is called a glorification. This may take the form of added decorative carvings or inlays, and it may even involve re-turning or recarving bedposts or table and chair legs. A glorification is spotted only by signs of modern workmanship and tools and by your own knowledge of the style and design of the period in question.

By way of summary, it should be emphasized that *value* is a fluctuating and intangible thing. Whether a piece is authentic or bogus, its value is determined jointly by the buyer and the seller. Even the honest dealer, who will not knowingly misrepresent a piece, will charge whatever the market will bear. Some dealers put firm prices on their wares and are not open to negotiation; others put the prices they hope to get and are happy indeed when a customer pays without question.

The information that has been presented in this and the preceding chapters will help you separate the antiques from the fakes as you study and gain experience in this field. Many antique dealers get into this business because they like antiques and they are knowledgeable about them. Most of them will be glad to share their knowledge with you and help you learn to appreciate old pieces fully.

17

How to Spend and Save at Auctions

An auction is a fascinating and exciting marketplace that is like no other. It is an excellent source of old and antique furniture. An auction is a place where some people get occasional "steals," while more get "stuck." In either case, an auction is more interesting and more fun than any other marketplace. After one or two exposures many people become auction buffs or addicts or nuts. Perhaps this is because of the open competition or perhaps because of the unpredictable outcome.

Have you ever bought a piece for a small fraction of its value? If it was from a dealer or an owner, you probably had something of a guilty conscience. If it was at an auction, the result was pure exhilaration; you had gotten the "best" of dozens or hundreds of people! Every auction addict likes to tell stories of his shrewdness.

More often there are other stories that you will not hear. Those are the stories of getting stuck—of paying much more than an item is worth. You can see it happen time and again at any auction. If you don't see it, you don't hear about it because people don't like to boast of overpaying. Frequently, they never even know they have done it!

These things happen at every auction. The reasons are twofold. First, the buyer must know the merchandise, and that is what several earlier chapters were about. Secondly, the auction is a highly specialized marketplace. The buyer must know how it operates and how to make its psychology work for him instead of against him.

This chapter is for those who have never attended an auction and, thus, missed out on this outstanding source of furniture. It is also for those who have attended auctions but who have lost out more than they have won. The information here will not guarantee a "steal" or even a bargain every time, but it should enable you to make the win-lose ratio more favorable.

There are several types of auctions. Some are by mail. Some are by sealed bids, opened on the spot or at a later time. We shall be concerned with the type that requires personal, open bidding where buyers compete on the spot for each article. This is the type most frequently held, and it is much more fun than the others.

All such auctions have a great deal in common whether they are backyard auctions, estate auctions, dealers' auctions, or benefit auctions.

It is easy to find auctions. In some parts of the country during the spring, summer, and fall, all you have to do is to get in the car on a Saturday and start driving. You will find several, but this is a haphazard way of doing it. Perhaps the best way is to watch for advertisements in newspapers, especially those serving smaller or more rural areas. They usually carry more auction ads than the big-city papers. Small-town papers always have ads for local sales, and a twenty-five or fifty-mile drive to a good auction can be very worthwhile. On a good day, such papers will frequently offer two or three auctions from which to choose.

Many big cities and smaller communities have one or more auction houses that hold scheduled sales weekly or more frequently. Newspapers and yellow pages often carry their ads. Sometimes such sales are not advertised because "everyone" knows about them. A little detective work—a few questions here and there—will often turn them up in nearby communities.

A frequently overlooked source of auction information is the auctioneers themselves. Every area has its auctioneers who work on a commission basis. They will almost always notify you of the place and time of each of their auctions, especially if you give them stamped, self-addressed envelopes. Often they will send a listing of the articles to be auctioned. After all, this is good business for them; the more people who attend their auctions, the more money they will make.

Having found an auction, you will make preparations to attend. Of course, the basic preparation is your continuing study of furniture and refinishing so that you can separate the wheat from the chaff. You should dress appropriately, especially for the rural-type auction.

Ladies will wish to wear slacks in order to be more comfortable while shifting, turning, and examining furniture.

Most rural-type sales are held outside or in drafty sheds or barns. Cold weather can become very penetrating in four or five hours; this calls for boots, heavy coats, and gloves. Hot sun can become quite uncomfortable, requiring a brimmed hat, sunglasses, and long sleeves. You may need boots because of yesterday's rain. You may need an umbrella for today's drizzle that is not serious enough to cause postponement of the sale. A small folding camp stool can prove most useful in some situations. Do not forget to carry your inspection tool kit described earlier.

Though it depends somewhat on the type of auction, you should plan to arrive on the scene about an hour before the scheduled starting time. Your purpose is to examine the articles that will be offered. Sometimes the articles are available for examination before the day of the sale, but it is an unwritten rule that they open up at least an hour early.

Regardless of when you do it, however, examine in detail every item in which you are seriously interested. Obviously, the more money involved, the more detailed the examination should be, because you won't get a second chance. At most sales, when the auctioneer says "sold," the item is yours for better or for worse.

We have said several times that an examination should be thorough. Let us examine a small chest together so you can see how it is done. First, we look at the obvious things: Is it sturdy and tight or about to fall apart? Are any pieces missing or damaged beyond repair? Is the hardware complete and is it original? Has the chest been mistreated? Are there surface damages? Can all damages be repaired and is it worthwhile?

After this gross examination, we look closer: Is the piece veneer or solid wood? What kind of wood? Have any parts been replaced? Are the drawer joints tight? Are dovetails the type expected? Are drawer bottoms shrunken? Runners and sides worn? Tool marks visible? Proper type nails or screws? Does the evidence match the reputed age of the piece?

Of course, all during the examination we have been observing and evaluating the finish: What is it? Is it original? Can it be restored? Is complete refinishing necessary?

That's the way we conduct an inspection. At first it is a rather lengthy process. As you gain experience, however, you can examine a piece fairly quickly. Of course, with a piece of special interest or worth, the examination is much more detailed, including, for example, the use of rule and calipers to measure shrinkage.

The entire purpose of inspecting the piece is to decide whether or not we want it. If we do, we decide immediately what it is worth or what our top price will be.

Now, this is where a lot of people go wrong at auctions. They fail to set a top price for themselves before the bidding starts, and that is exactly what the auctioneer is counting on to get high prices. He counts on your competitive spirit and the excitement to take you up, up, and *away!*

This is quite likely to happen if you do not set a top price for yourself and stick to it unless overwhelming evidence indicates that you should raise it. In addition to the excitement and competition, the auctioneer's logic can get to you, too. When he says, "It's just one more dollar," that sounds good every time he says it. It sounds good, that is, until you have to plunk down $80 for a chest that is not worth a penny more than $55.

Getting back to the examination of the chest—or clock or table or chair or whatever it was—you must carry out your inspection as casually as possible. Try not to be too intense. Be unobtrusive about it. Don't look pleased with what you discover. When you finish your examination, walk away shaking your head sadly.

Does this sound like play-acting? You bet it is, and there is more to come. Do not return to the item you want, to caress or check it again. Move around and examine closely several articles in which you have no interest unless they are being given away. And look pleased as you inspect a piece you don't want.

You have the idea now? Sure. Lead a false trail. Do not let anyone discover your intentions ahead of time.

Often there are shills or friends of the auctioneer circulating and watching the customers' examinations. These business partners of the auctioneer are good practical psychologists and they can tell when someone wants something. The shills' job, then, is to run up the price when the bidding starts. They do it quite well.

Let us give you an example: Not too long ago we were checking a few items before an auction when we noticed a young couple examining and exclaiming over an old hall rack. They gave it a good going-over, talking excitedly to each other all the while. A "friend of the house" was taking it all in also. Well, the couple finally left the hall rack, but they came back to it several times before the sale started. It was obvious what was going to happen.

The auction started, and finally the hall rack was put up. The couple started bidding immediately. They could hardly wait to top an opposing bid. Soon, other bidders dropped out and the couple was bidding only against the shill. On and on they went until the shill exercised his second great talent and dropped out when he had pushed the couple just as high as he figured he could.

So the couple got the hall rack by paying nearly three times the price that the house had hoped to get. Well, the couple was happy, and maybe that's what counts.

This is an extreme example, but it is a true one. You see how it can happen, and that's the reason for the play-acting.

You may be wondering what happens if the shill misjudges and pushes the price too high and the customer drops out. This doesn't happen very often, for these people are very good; but sometimes it does. It's no great thing; the house simply keeps it and puts it up another day.

The skillful auctioneer will sometimes do this same sort of thing alone. When he gets a real live bidder, he acknowledges a few fictitious bids to push the price up a few dollars more. So disguise your interest from the time you walk in until you leave.

Occasionally we hear concern expressed about dealers going to auctions. You really have nothing to fear from us when you find us at a sale. We don't drive the bidding up. Think about it for a minute. We can't stay in the bidding when it gets anywhere near the value of an item because we have to resell it. If we pay near market value and add our expenses and add a reasonable profit margin, the article would be way overpriced in the shop and we'd be stuck with it. So don't worry about the dealers present; they will stop at 50 to 75 percent of value, and you can still get a bargain. Your pocketbook is one question, but from the standpoint of value you can always top a dealer's bid. The shoe is really on the other foot; we are afraid of you at auctions because *you* drive the prices up!

Some people use dealers' knowledge of market value to their own advantage. They watch the dealers' bidding and know that they can go at least a little higher without getting stuck. How do you spot the dealers? They are the fellows—usually fellows but sometimes gals—who attend auctions regularly. You'll see those who go at most of them. They are the ones who, on good days, buy more than someone would want simply to put in his own home. Then, too, they are the people at auctions who often look bored with the whole thing —even when they are bidding!

Well, now, you have examined the chest and decided on your top price of $65, and the time has come. The auctioneer points to the chest and says something like, "What am I bid? Who will start it at fifty dollars?"

Don't say a word! Don't even breathe! Just hope that some other idiot doesn't start it at $50 either. The reason is quite simple. We would like to have just one dollar for every time we have seen someone start the bidding at the auctioneer's first asking figure, then there were no more bids. The first one was the last one. Who knows what lower figure it might have sold for?

So don't you start it at $50. If you do, and there are no more bids, you will never know but what you might have gotten it for $40 or $25. Don't be anxious. Let someone else start it if he will. There will be plenty of opportunity for you to bid if you want to.

If he gets no bid after asking for $50 several times, the auctioneer may say, "All right. Who wants it at forty?" If he still gets no takers, he will keep dropping until a bid starts it out.

The bidding may get started in another way. When the auctioneer asked for a starting bid of $50, someone may have said, "Twenty-five." This is the one time when you may bid lower than the auctioneer's figure. He may accept it and start the bidding there, or he may not.

So the bidding starts at some figure less than your maximum. What do you do now? Just stay quiet awhile—give others a chance to bid. There is a lot of psychology in every phase of this auction sale.

Let them start it at, say, $25 and let them bat it around as long as they want to. If they pass your top figure, you haven't lost anything anyway. Then, too, if you get in the early bidding, it adds to your opponents' excitement and may cause them to go even higher. So let them toss it back and forth until one finally thinks that he has it.

Now, if you, who haven't said a word, pop up and take it from him, he is very discouraged. Here he has just beaten another fellow and you come out of nowhere to beat him. Your strategy is that he will be so surprised and discouraged that he will quit—and sometimes it happens that way.

Well, you are ready to make your first bid. Do anything that will attract the auctioneer's attention. We are continually amazed at how many people think that there are secret bidding signals or that there is some certain way of bidding. There is no special way to bid—just attract the auctioneer's attention. You may wave your hand, say "Here," state your figure, nod your head, or just grunt! *Just get his attention!* He knows what you are there for and why you want him, and that is to bid the price he is asking.

Auctioneers are very alert people. You may have to be a little violent with your wave or raise your voice extra loud when you first enter a bidding series, but once he spots you, you are in. If your bid is then topped, he will look back directly at you to see what you want to do. Then even a slight nod of the head yea or nay will suffice. Of course, it is perfectly acceptable to continue to bid with a wave or by voice. In fact, a voice bid may sometimes help demoralize your opponent.

There is another tactic that may be effective on your opponent when there are just the two of you bidding. That is to hesitate so long that he thinks he has it, but throw in your bid just before the auctioneer gives it to him. Of course, this may also be interpreted as a sign that you are weakening, so be careful about overplaying it.

This discussion of bidding signals should tell you something else, too. Don't yell or wave at a friend at an auction. You may find that you have bought a plastic birdbath for twice its regular price at the dime store.

If you go to an auction with your husband or wife, keep together or, at least, tell each other what you're going to bid on. It is very embarrassing and expensive to discover suddenly that you are bidding against your spouse. It happened to us on one occasion that we *know* of because the auctioneer generously said, "That bid came from your better half. Are you sure you want to top it?"

As if that were not bad enough, just wait until you bid against yourself and the auctioneer says, "That thirty-one dollars is your bid, Savage. Why are you trying to bid thirty-two?"

The moral is that an auction can get hectic from time to time, but you must try to keep up with everything that is going on. You won't always be able to, but try. You can *watch* an auction with half of your attention, but *participating* in one that way can be very costly.

Listen very carefully to the auctioneer as he puts up each item. The words he says can be very significant:

"By the piece, for the pair" means that you are bidding on two items, a pair of them, but the bid price is for each one. So if you bid $15 on a pair of $20 candlesticks, you will pay $30 for the two, which you are obligated to take.
"All for one money" means that you are bidding a price for the lot.
"By the piece" means that, even though there is a pair or a set of the items, you are bidding on just one of them.
"By the piece, one or more" means that you are bidding on one of a pair or a set. However, you will have the privilege of taking the one or as many of them as you want at the same price each.
"By the piece, for the set" means that you will have to take all the matching items at the "each" price you bid. If the set consists of eight dining chairs and you bid $20, you must pay $160 and take all of them.

So you must listen carefully to avoid a costly mistake or, perhaps, to get a good bargain. And if you are unsure of the conditions, stop the auctioneer and ask. Most of them are honest fellows and want you to know what you are bidding on.

Now, the auctioneer may be honest, but he is no fool. Watch out for any description that he gives of the item. Nearly all local auctioneers will give honest descriptions, but they are under no obligation to draw you a picture. Listen carefully; he means just what he says —no more and no less. For example, if he says, "It looks old," that's what he means: It *looks* old. It may or may not *be* old. He didn't say it was, and you must use your judgment on that.

"Jake says this chest is at least a hundred and fifty years old." Sure, Jake said that, but who is Jake? Does he really know, and is *he* honest? "This pitcher sure looks like cutglass" can really drive the price up if there are a couple of unwary bidders around. Or someone in the crowd asks what kind of wood a table is made of, and the auctioneer says, "It looks like walnut." It may be and then again it may be pine with a walnut finish; he hasn't said what it is.

Well, you can easily see that the biggest secret of the successful auction-enthusiast is to *be alert.* It is for him that the Romans invented the expression *caveat emptor.* "Let the buyer beware," they said, "because he should not be ignorant of the property that he is buying." Do your bidding with both eyes and ears open.

At no time is this maxim more applicable than when an old trunk or box is auctioned "as found, unopened." Now, even if the auctioneer and owner (whoever he may be) and all their helpers are honest, this does not automatically mean that the trunk contains something of value. It may, but then, too, it may be full of packing paper or five-year-old paperback books. In any case, your reaction to such an old trunk will depend on your pocketbook and your sense of adventure or, if you prefer, your gambling spirit.

Surely you have heard of people finding valuable old stamps or jewelry or first editions or Presidents' autographs in such purchases. Far more people, though you never hear about them, find absolutely nothing of value. Yet, who knows, this could be *the one,* and it's just a few dollars.

We could tell you several true stories of what we have found among the assorted junk in such boxes and trunks. In all honesty, however, we have taken nearly all of them to the trash just as we brought them from the auction. This must be impulse buying in its most primitive form!

By all means, do not feel that you must get something at every auction you attend. Many people feel that way, and they pay for it in unwanted or overpriced merchandise. You have *not* wasted your time if you go home empty-handed. Every auction adds to your knowledge of values, prices, styles, and even of auction psychology. Besides, attending auctions is great *fun.*

Sooner or later, however, you will make the last and highest bid on an item. When this happens, the bookkeeper will want to know who bought it, so he or the auctioneer will ask.

At some auctions each person who intends to bid signs up and is given a number. If the number is on a card about 6" × 9", hold it up so that the bookkeeper can see it. If not, call out your assigned number to the auctioneer or bookkeeper. Where a number system is not used, just call out your name.

Then the auctioneer goes on with the next article. Meanwhile, depending on the formality of the auction, the item you purchased will be placed aside with your name or number on it. Other items will be added as you purchase them. Small items may be sent or passed to where you are sitting or standing, and once they are in your possession they are your responsibility.

Usually you do not pay for each item as you get it. At the end of the auction or whenever you are ready to leave, the cashier totals your purchases and takes your payment. Cash is always acceptable. Personal checks *may* be accepted if you are known or properly identified. National charge cards are accepted at many auctions. If you wish to use check or card, it is wise to inquire before the auction.

Your final task is to get your purchases home. Very few auctions provide delivery service, but some will arrange it for a fee. Many will provide assistance in getting your large purchases loaded into your car, trailer, or truck. If you have bought more than you can carry, you can frequently arrange to leave some (at your own risk, of course) until you can get them.

You will notice that we have said nothing about deciphering the auctioneer's "chant." Don't be frightened off by the tobacco auctioneer on television; he is dealing with professional buyers. Those working with the public don't sound like that. They work fast but not so fast that you can't understand them. Then, too, if you do lose track of the bidding, you can always stop him and ask what he is asking.

One final point about auctions: When you make the final bid, the item is yours for better or worse. Very rarely have we seen auctioneers willing to take back an item after it is sold. They usually will if there has been an honest misunderstanding. If the buyer has made a careless error, such as his original estimate of the condition of the piece, the auctioneer usually will not take it back. We have seen that happen when prodded by the buyer and when necessary to keep the good will of the crowd—but no further bids from that individual were acknowledged. So take the last bid and take the item. If you make a mistake, charge it up to the cost of learning.

Over the long run, auctions are the best source of old and antique furniture for the home refinisher. Only those who wholesale to dealers can provide better buys, and that source is closed to you. If you have never attended an auction, hesitate no longer. Look up a few. You may become an addict!

Good luck on your buying and your refinishing.

18

Starting a Refinishing Business

Many home refinishers eventually find their way into commercial refinishing. Some do so quite deliberately, while for others it is an unplanned, accidental process. As your refinishing proficiency increases through doing your own pieces, you may find yourself in the business or desiring to get into it. In most areas of the country there is plenty of opportunity. We will discuss in this chapter the basics of starting a refinishing business.

Why People Get into the Business

Probably more amateurs get into commercial refinishing by accident than by design. It sort of creeps up on them and they begin in self-defense. Frequently it happens something like this:

You take up refinishing and go your merry way deriving enjoyment and satisfaction making your home come alive with beautiful old pieces. Your relatives, friends, and acquaintances admire your handiwork greatly. Suddenly you find yourself doing one of two things: Either you are refinishing someone else's piece "as a favor" or you are becoming increasingly uncomfortable at having to continually refuse to "help" a relative or friend.

This is not an imaginary situation. It happens time and again. Until you begin refinishing you wouldn't believe that every household contains one or a dozen pieces that are crying to be redone. The owners don't know how to begin or they wouldn't dare attempt it on their "good" pieces, and commercial refinishers are *so* expensive. And there you are, caught in the middle.

176

Now, these good folk would not think of asking their friend the dairyman for a free supply of milk or their friend the painter for a free house painting or their other friends for a suit or a car or a lawn mowing. Yet *you*—you do such good work; you're such a good friend; you're not in business!

So you go into business to protect yourself from relatives, friends, and acquaintances (the gall of some people!). Other and more practical reasons for refinishing commercially are to earn money for the purchase of more furniture for yourself or to get rid of excess pieces we all acquire. Many people do so in order to supplement their regular income or just to earn "playing" money. Some get into the business simply to have something to occupy their time or perhaps to feel useful—to improve their self-concept. Still others start a part-time business in order to "test the water" for a possible full-time venture. Whatever your reason, in most places you can do as much or as little as you like—from a few pieces a year to a few pieces a week.

Types of Businesses

When you start refinishing on a commercial basis, you may go in one of two main directions. The first, obviously, is to provide services only. In this case, you refinish or restore pieces for the owners for a fee. You sell a service, not a product.

The other main road you can choose to travel is to sell pieces you have refinished. In essence, you will be setting up an "antique shop" type of business. Generally, the beginner in a venture of this sort sells only periodically. When he has built up a small supply of finished pieces he sells them off and starts building a new supply. Often he specializes in a particular type of piece: tables, chests, chairs, or the like. This refinisher was once known as "the table lady" by auctioneers and dealers alike. We purchased, refinished, and resold mostly tables when we discovered that there was quite a demand. Every home has at least one spot that calls for an occasional table of one sort or another.

Most commercial ventures operate in both streams, however. They offer refinishing services and, at the same time, keep a few pieces on hand to sell. You may choose the direction or combination that most appeals to you and for which there is a need in your community.

How to Get Started

The first requirement for starting a business is that you learn to refinish *well*. While many potential customers will be satisfied with mediocre workmanship, the discriminating buyer will not put up with it. Of course, the money and the repeat business is in the discriminating buyer, but there is more involved than that. You must develop the skills that will enable you to have justifiable pride in your work. If you are not proud of your work, how can your customer take pride in owning and showing it? Never turn any piece out unless you would be happy to have it in your own home.

As we have indicated, a business will often start itself with little or no effort on your part. Potential customers will begin to seek you out as they see or hear of your work. In this era when very high prices and very low-quality workmanship seem to be the rule, personal recommendation is probably the best advertising medium. The word gets around remarkably fast among people who are interested in old furniture. It gets around the bridge table, the golf course, and the circle meeting.

You can give the process a boost in several ways. Let your friends and acquaintances know that you are doing or will do refinishing for others or that you have several pieces exceeding your needs or space. This can be done quite casually: You are not soliciting their business particularly; you just want the word to get out.

At times when someone is admiring your work he will mention that he has an unused piece in the attic or garage. Often he will be delighted with your offer to refinish a piece for him in exchange for the unused one. Such a trade will benefit you in two ways. First, you acquire a piece that you can refinish and keep or sell at a profit. Secondly, you will gain advertising value, since your name will probably be mentioned when a friend of your friend expresses admiration of the piece you refinished "in trade."

Low-cost newspaper ads can bring a flood of calls even in relatively small communities. Typically, an occasional well-worded ad will bring as much business as you care to handle. You will probably be surprised at the response to

---

FOR SALE: a few refinished pieces, antique and old. Occasional tables, oak sideboard, mahogany chest, trunk. Call 123–4567.

---

or

FURNITURE REFINISHING: top workmanship, reasonable cost, pickup and delivery. Get that old piece redone today. Call 123–4567.

Of course, there are other ways to sell your products. In many sections of the country *yard* or *garage* sales have caught on. Such a sale may be put on by an individual or by a small group of neighbors or friends. You can have your own yard sale or join with others.

The basic procedure is quite simple. Advertise in your local paper that a yard sale will be held at a stated time and place. You may wish to list a few items or, at least, give an idea of the type or types of items that will be available. Prior to the time of the sale, have everything ready, because there are usually "eager beavers" who arrive early to get the jump on other buyers. Have your furniture pieces priced and on display in the garage, yard, or basement. Have some change on hand; it is sad to lose a sale for lack of a five and a couple of ones.

A yard sale is a good way to make more space for your refinishing. Sell off the stuff that is cluttering up your work or storage space. Put it out with a price tag whether it is good junk or junk junk. Remember, one man's trash is another's gold mine. People will buy just about anything, especially if they think it is a "bargain." One final point: If at all possible, keep out of sight anything that you do not want to sell. You may find that someone has bought your good charcoal grill in the excitement.

Another interesting and effective way of selling your pieces is at auction. Of course, you may hold your own, but an auction is more complex to arrange than a yard sale. We would advise beginners to work with experienced auctioneers. You can have an auctioneer hold a sale for you if you have a reasonable quantity of items. He will charge a 10 to 20 percent commission on sales, but he takes care of everything. Get a *good* auctioneer. He charges you no more; he will have a "following" of auction addicts; and he will often get you sufficiently higher prices to more than pay his commission.

With few or many items, you may wish to work through established auction sales. Many communities, large and small, have so-called auction houses that hold regularly scheduled sales. Often a civic club will sponsor regular sales. These operate on a commission basis like the independent auctioneers. Check on their terms and rules about allowing minimum prices to be set, for example. You can deliver your pieces to the sale or they will pick up for a fee.

Buying for Resale

In order to sustain even a part-time business, you must maintain your stock. Often you will buy a piece with the thought of selling it to a specific person. "Jean Jones said the other day that she had been looking for a square oak table." Seldom, however, will anyone guarantee to buy a piece if you can find one for him. He wants to see it first, and so would you. Thus you must have some stock, even though small at first. You must buy on speculation and replenish your stock as you make sales.

If you plan to operate on a small-scale, occasional basis, your buying can function the same way. As you visit sources listed in Chapters 14 and 17 for your personal purchases, you can pick up "extra" pieces when you find them particularly attractive and/or low-cost. When you have acquired and refinished several, you can have a sale. This does have two disadvantages if you allow your business to grow beyond the occasional stage. First, the type and rate of acquisitions will be unpredictable and, second, your costs will be fairly high, leaving you little margin for profit. And profit is necessary. You must cover costs—the cost of the piece, the cost of refinishing supplies, and the cost of transportation. In addition you must cover other items—the value of your "shopping" and buying time, your refinishing time, and your bookkeeping time. And then some profit. Obviously, you must buy as low as possible.

There are other sources of stock you should investigate and develop as your turnover increases. There are pickers and/or wholesalers whose business is supplying dealers' needs. Some are interested in relatively small-volume operations. You will have to find out how to contact local wholesalers from a friendly fellow dealer. Their prices are generally right but, as in all business transactions, keep a sharp eye open.

Within fifty miles or so of most communities there are periodic dealers' sales or auctions. Usually they are held during a weekday so that they won't be bothered with the general public. Sometimes only bona fide dealers are admitted. Most welcome new dealers. Again, these are not publicly advertised, so you will have to learn about them from established dealers.

By this time you probably have decided that the antique/old-furniture business is quite different from other types of business. Now we will prove it to you. Active dealers do a lot of buying from and selling to each other. It is not unusual for a piece to go through three or four dealers before a consumer buys it for his home. It is an inside joke among dealers that they sell mostly to each other. One dealer's price to another may be anywhere between 10 percent above cost to 10 percent below "retail." As a dealer, you can expect such prices, but once again keep your eyes open wide. Dealers haggle and bargain among themselves much more than they do with customers.

We should remind you, however, that the dealer who *first* buys a piece from its consumer-owner gets it for the lowest price and, thereby, stands to make the greatest profit. It is for this reason that your best sources of supply financially are the least dependable for constancy and volume of supply. Newspaper ads ("Wanted: old furniture . . .") and yard sales are your best bet since they frequently turn up good pieces at low cost. Public auctions are generally not too good for dealers for reasons mentioned in an earlier chapter. You can pick up bargains at public auctions when you find one poorly attended or when you discover pieces that look like junk but to your knowledgeable eye are easily repairable.

Refinishing in Quantity

Some home refinishers start a part-time business and never seem to be able to get beyond the "occasional" stage. Those who wish to but can't often don't know how and where to buy, or how to advertise and sell, or how to price their goods. Some can't make it simply because they continue to refinish just as they did when they were doing just their own pieces.

As the business grows, the sheer volume of refinishing exceeds the capacity of the one-person, one-piece operation. The processes remain the same, but techniques must be modified. This does not imply any decrease in the *quality* of your work—it must not. You must never lose sight of the fact that it is the *high quality* of your service and product that sets you apart from and above a dozen other refinisher/dealers. You can increase capacity while maintaining quality. There are several guidelines for doing so.

First, increase your efficiency. Stop taking one piece from stripping to dressing before beginning another. Work on several pieces together. Carrying three or four pieces (or more) through the refinishing processes together will save a great deal of getting ready, putting away, and cleaning-up time. Learn to think in terms of processes rather than pieces.

Stripping-to-dressing time on a candle table may run a couple of days if you do it alone. You will spend much less time on it if you refinish it right along with a lowboy or hutch, for example. The more pieces you do simultaneously, the more time you save. The only practical limitation to this increased efficiency is the space in which you work.

As you move into this type of operation don't get yourself in a bind. Before, you could promise a customer that his piece would be ready in three days or four. Now you will have to allow yourself more time so that you can do several pieces, saving some time on each one but taking longer for them all. The other pieces may be some to refinish or some that you have been holding back to have for sale when needed or that you then go out and buy to refinish. Of course, they may also be pieces brought in by other customers.

The second guideline for quantity refinishing is to get yourself some help. It is obvious that two people can turn out more work than one. Even a part-time business can use part-time help. Part-time or full-time, you will have to teach them their duties, but things are not that complicated. You furnish the brains and some muscle; your "assistant" furnishes only muscle, at least at first. In most communities, part-time workers are easy to locate.

There are always high-school students looking for part-time jobs, and most of them make good employees. Typically, they are available for work in the late afternoons and on weekends. An excellent source of part-time student workers is one of the work-study cooperative programs found in many high schools. For example, Industrial Cooperative Training (ICT) students are released from school a part of each day to go to work. They generally work fifteen to twenty hours a week for which they are paid (by you) and for which they are granted credit toward graduation (by the school). The guidance counselor at your local high school can help you get in touch with co-op students or others interested in employment.

Community colleges and other institutions in your vicinity are also good sources of part-time employees. The college placement office can be of help to you in making contacts.

The third quantity guideline has more to do with finances than with time. Certain savings in supplies will result from your refinishing several pieces together rather than one at a time. As your quantity increases, however, you can cut your expenses significantly by the way you purchase those supplies.

In the "occasional" stage it is likely that you will have to be satisfied with the 10 to 20 percent discount you can get from most paint and hardware stores. A commercial discount of, say, 15 percent is not to be disdained. That will save you quite a bit per year on stripper, steel wool, stain, varnish, brushes, and the like.

As your business grows, so will your supply needs. Sooner or later you reach the stage where you can buy in quantity great enough to interest a wholesaler or distributor. Then your savings can be quite good. Perhaps a local store will help you locate and get in touch with his distributor. If not, contact the various manufacturers of the supplies you use (read the labels). They will send you the name of their local distributor and/or have their own sales representative call on you.

Transportation

When you enter the refinishing or dealer or combination business, you will be faced with the problem of transportation. Pieces, whether yours or the customers', must be moved to and from your shop. You can, of course, simply provide none for customers—they have to bring it in and pick it up as best they can. While such a policy will work, it is certain that it will cut down on your potential business. Even a station wagon will not hold a moderately large piece of furniture. You should be able to provide transportation. In addition, you will need a means for transporting to your shop those pieces that you purchase. You can do this in several ways.

A station wagon and/or a flat car-top carrier are quite limited in capacity and are inconvenient to use for any but the smallest pieces. You could get by with this at first by supplementing with the renting of a trailer when greater capacity is needed. Nearly every community is served by one or more national rental agencies, such as U-Haul, Hertz, or Nationwide. Then, too, many rental stores can provide trailers.

You will soon discover that rental trailers do not come cheap. A few rentals (about a dozen at this writing) and you have spent enough to buy a trailer of your own. This is the reason why we consider the purchase of a trailer advisable for all but the smallest operations. This could be your first purchase with your business profits.

A four-foot by six- or eight-foot trailer will handle all but the largest pieces, yet be relatively inexpensive. Take note of the word *relatively*. In our section of the country a good trailer of any size is *not* inexpensive. However, if you take your time looking and advertising, you should be able to find something for about twelve times the rental rate. We prefer one with three- or four-foot sides and no top. A fixed top will limit the height of pieces you can carry. Obviously, a good tarp is necessary.

Perhaps a pickup truck is the best all-around furniture transporter. Trucks, even used ones, are quite expensive. You could justify such a purchase only for a full-time business, though there are other justifications for buying a pickup truck. There is another disadvantage to using a truck: It won't ride as comfortably as your car. On a long buying trip, that can make a difference, especially if the whole family is going along to combine business and pleasure.

You probably have noticed that we have not mentioned the possibility of borrowing a trailer or truck. If you are involved in a business venture, borrowing transportation is highly inadvisable. When the friend from whom you borrow realizes that you are making money with his truck or trailer, he is likely to become less friendly. Friends are too hard to come by to risk losing them in this manner. Despite your first thought, the solution is *not* to rent his trailer or truck. Most people do not carry the right type of insurance or licenses on their personal, noncommercial vehicles. In case of an accident, you and he could lose your shirts.

The solution is to rent from a commercial leasor, pay to have your pieces transported, or buy your own vehicle. The charge you make for delivery or the slightly higher price on your pieces will pay for your trailer sooner or later.

Pricing

As a beginning commercial refinisher/dealer you will probably encounter difficulty in trying to decide how to price your products and services. We can provide only some general guidance, since prices vary so greatly from one section of the country to another.

You may use the approach to pricing that a number of dealers use. These misguided souls have a vague feeling for market value but base their prices almost entirely on their costs. The amount they paid for the piece, plus an amount for their trouble, including any work the piece required, plus an amount for profit equals the price they ask. This is a very haphazard method that depends too much on what they pay for their stock. Often their shops will contain some pieces that are underpriced and some that are overpriced. These are usually marginal shops that barely manage to stay in business, hoping for better times.

Our recommendation is that you price your goods and services a little more scientifically. Here are some general principles to guide you:

1. *For the most part, ignore published "Antiques Price Lists."* First, identification of pieces is often difficult. Second, the value of a piece varies greatly, depending on its condition. Third, value depends on location. A difference of only one hundred miles, to say nothing of two thousand miles, can make a marked difference in the market value of a piece.

2. *Keep in touch with prices being charged by others in your area.* This is your best general guide to pricing your goods and services. Do some comparison shopping, checking both prices and quality. Talk with other dealers in their shops and at sales. Watch the

prices they *pay* at sales. Watch where they drop out of the bidding at public auctions. These factors will provide you with a base on which to make your own price decisions.

3. *Keep in mind what you offer the customer—custom service and quality workmanship.* Do not hesitate to charge more than the mediocre-and-worse charge. If customers want their pieces dipped white and fuzzy, let them do so with your blessing. (They may even discover the meaning of the sign "Not responsible for veneer or glue . . ." Often these pieces will be returned to you for repair and/or refinishing—to your greater profit.) If customers want their pieces finished sloppily with runs or, worse, with sprayed lacquer (with or without runs), let them go elsewhere. Send on with a smile those folk who don't care if their pieces are sanded or planed(!). You may quake inside to see a good piece so treated, but it is theirs to do with as they will.

Not everyone appreciates a first-class car, and not all those who do can afford one. So it is with refinishing. Your main product is quality and custom service. Charge accordingly and realize that you will lose some business thereby. (What would you do if you had *all* the business, anyway?) New business people sometimes feel that their prices must be as low as or lower than everyone else's prices. Not so. Do not hesitate to charge more than the mediocre competition—provided, of course, that you *do* provide the quality they do not.

On the other end of the spectrum, you wouldn't believe the prices charged by the well-known quality refinishers. There are not many of these businesses around, and they have more work than they can do. They charge accordingly. When you are starting out, your costs will be less than theirs and you can afford to charge less. We suggest that you set your prices somewhere between those of the run-of-the-mill fellow and those of the quality refinisher/dealer *if* you can find one in your area.

Miscellaneous Business Pointers

As your business activities increase you will need some means of identification. Choose a name for your enterprise and have some stationery and cards printed. A letterhead or a business card will identify you in almost any situation. For example, one of these is generally all that is needed to establish your eligibility for commercial discounts or wholesale buying.

If your business is a part-time one, you may not wish to be available at any and all hours. You may establish specific days and/or hours and put this information on your business material. If you want to retain greater flexibility, put "By Appointment Only" on your letterheads and cards, as in the examples shown.

Offer your clients custom service as well as quality workmanship. Do not fall into the habit of putting the same finish on everything. Not all pieces require, nor should they receive, the same finish. Explain the options, such as opaque/clear or varnish/shellac/lacquer, make a recommendation, and then do what the customer wants unless you know that it would be unsatisfactory. He should have the option of leaving the dark rings in the top or replacing a missing decorative

Handcrafted

FURNITURE REFINISHING

J. D. Savage

By appointment

FRANKLIN ☐☐☐ ☐☐☐☐

CONGRATULATIONS! You have just acquired a fine, handcrafted furniture <u>finish</u>. It is one which will provide many years of superb service if it is given a minimal amount of proper care.

You may think it strange to speak of the finish in the manner usually used to speak of design, wood, or structure. The truth is, however, that the finish on a piece of wooden furniture is just as important as the design or wood, itself, but it is much less observable. Even a novice can quickly learn to evaluate the design of a piece and the wood from which it is constructed. On the other hand, the expert can seldom be certain of all the qualities of a finish unless he has applied it himself. We assume that you know what you have in terms of wood and structure; we want to assure you that you have a <u>finish</u> of the highest quality.

TYPE OF FINISH

While there is an almost infinite variety of finishes, we use only proven materials and processes of three basic types. The particular type used in each instance is selected on the basis of the age and condition of the piece, its intended use, and, of course, the owner's preference. These types and their characteristics are listed below and the one which you have acquired is checked.

☐ HAND-RUBBED OIL   Several coats of an especially prepared oil have been individually worked into the surface of the wood. There is no appearance or feeling of oiliness in this velvety finish of medium hardness. It is often suited to fine antiques which will not be subjected to hard use. The hand-rubbed oil finish has already been topped with wax (see Maintenance, below).

☐ VARNISH   After the surface has been suitably prepared (a sealer and a body-building preparation), a final varnish-type finish is applied. This combination of materials produces a very hard, water- and alcohol-proof finish. Proper rubdown of each coat produces both an exceptionally smooth surface and one of the desired degree of gloss. Thus, this finish may vary from dull, through satin, to high gloss. This, too, has been dressed with an application of wax (see Maintenance, below).

☐ SEALER FINISH   Occasionally it is desirable to use this smooth, dull, and relatively fragile finish on a piece. After the wood surface has been suitably prepared, a special sealer is applied and rubbed down. This is followed by a generous wax dressing.

MAINTENANCE

Each piece which we refinish is given a final dressing of hard wax before it leaves the shop. Unless the piece is to receive unusually heavy usage, it is unnecessary to apply additional wax before placing it in service.

Apart from normal dusting with a soft dry cloth, it is desirable to periodically run over at least the horizontal surfaces of the piece with a soft damp cloth followed by a briskly applied dry "re-polishing" cloth. We recommend that NO commercial liquid or spray polish or cleaner-polish be used on this (or any other) fine finish.

At intervals of approximately twelve months a new wax dressing should be applied. The specific timing of this operation will depend upon the amount of use the piece receives. First, the piece should be thoroughly cleaned usinga damp cloth, with or without mild soap, and immediately wiped dry. The idea is to remove the particles of dust and dirt which may have become embedded in the wax--not to remove the wax and, certainly, not to damage the finish beneath it. After the piece is thoroughly dry, a thin coat of any high quality paste wax may be used to re-dress the finish. Apply and polish the wax according to the manufacturer's instructions.

Proper maintenance as stated above will provide many years of service from your well-finished furniture. After a considerable time, however, you may find an objectionable wax build-up which mars the true beauty of the finish. This condition may be corrected by completely removing all the old wax and re-applying one such dressing. Old wax should be removed with great care in order to avoid damage to the finish. You should consider having a professional perform this operation on old, fine pieces.

REGISTRATION

The finish (and piece) which you have acquired has been coded, indexed, and completely recorded for your protection. Should it receive accidental damage in the future, we will be able to save you time and expense in its repair since we will know exactly what was used in the original finish.

J. D. Savage

part. It is, after all, his furniture and he has to live with it.

Provide every customer with printed instructions for the care of the finish he has purchased. This should be done whether the piece was brought in for refinishing or purchased from your refinished stock. A sample of a rather complete and versatile "care sheet" is given. Such a sheet costs little, yet builds a great deal of good will.

One final general pointer: If you are inexperienced in the business world, we suggest that you move into it slowly. Fortunately, no great expense need be incurred to get into the refinishing business on a part-time basis. You can start out slowly, risking little and testing the water as you go. As things develop, you can let the business itself dictate the need for expansion.

Legal Necessities

Even a small part-time business must meet certain legal requirements. As such requirements vary greatly from one locality to another and may become quite complex, we can only point out some of the areas that should be checked.

A business operated at your place of residence may fall under a variety of zoning regulations. Those can be checked with local officials as can the requirements, if any, for obtaining a business license. Many states and localities impose sales taxes on all or certain types of consumer purchases. You could be required to collect those taxes and forward them to appropriate agencies.

In many parts of the country school-age employees are required to have "work permits" issued by a local agency *for the specific job they will hold.* This requirement applies equally to part-time and full-time work. It is the responsibility of the employee to actually secure the permit, but it is the employer's obligation to have on file a permit for each affected worker.

Finally, there is the matter of record-keeping and taxes. Aside from requirements, you recognize the need for full and complete records of all disbursements and receipts. Without them you cannot know if you are making a profit, wasting your time, or losing your shirt. Records are necessary for tax purposes. The Internal Revenue Service will be quite helpful with advice and publications regarding the various types of taxes that may be applicable. You may have several options dealing with income, capital gains, and business profit (or loss). Don't forget FICA ("Social Security") requirements.

Of course, there is the matter of state and perhaps local taxes. These may be checked with local officials. If you do employ even one full- or part-time person, you must look into FICA and withholding requirements.

Dependent on your personal situation, the complexity of the requirements in your area, and the actual anticipated size of your business, it may be advisable for you to consult a lawyer or accountant knowledgeable in such matters.

Summary

There is a growing demand for refinishing services today. In some areas even mediocre workmanship is difficult if not impossible to find. The field is ripe for newcomers.

The public is becoming more aware of the various aspects of quality in refinishing. As this trend grows, the few refinishers who provide outstanding craftsmanship will become even more inaccessible.

If you are a *good* refinisher, if you can turn out a superior product, the chances are that the people in your area are looking for you. Your major problem may become how to take care of or refuse all the business that comes your way.

Despite this book or any other that may appear, most people won't do their own refinishing. Because of time or other factors they prefer to pay someone to do it for them. It might as well be you.

Glossary

Abrade. To rub a surface with a rough material, usually steel wool. Used to reduce gloss or to prepare a surface for a finish or to smooth it.

Alcohol, Denatured. A solvent for shellac used as a thinner, in testing, and in restoring shellac finishes.

Ammonia. Household ammonia is used for a number of purposes, such as remover for milk paint and as an ingredient of soda-ammonia remover for other finishes.

Antique. See Furniture, Antique.

Antique Oil. See Oil Finish.

Antiquing Kit. A commercially prepared kit of materials for applying a finish that is supposed to have the appearance of natural age.

Bleach. A substance that lightens the color of a surface to which it is applied.

Bleaching, Stain. Stains, accidental and deliberate, are bleached or removed by the application of liquid laundry bleach.

Bleaching, Wood. The natural color of wood is bleached or removed by the application of a commercial two-solution bleach.

Body. The thickness or depth of a clear finish.

Chisel. See Sandpaper.

Clamp. Any one of a number of devices used to temporarily hold two or more parts together tightly.

Clamp Sandwich. A "sandwich" consisting of scrap wood, waxed paper, glued joint, waxed paper, and scrap wood across which a clamp is attached.

Clear Finish. See Finish, Type: Clear.

Clorox. A brand name. See Bleaching, Stain.

Conversion. A piece that has been altered (converted) to resemble one that is more valuable.

Denatured Alcohol. See Alcohol, Denatured.

Dipping Tank. See Stripping Tank.

Dressing. The wax coating applied over a finish. Also the application of a wax coating.

Drop Cloth. A plastic cloth or paper sheet placed on a surface to protect it from damage by spattered or spilled liquids.

Enamel. Generally, a glossy paint.

End Grain. The grain (and appearance) on the end of a board that has been sawed across the grain or wood fibers.

Etch Mark. A mark in a surface made by some substance that has "eaten away" part of the surface—e.g., lemon juice on marble. An etch mark may or may not be discolored.

Exacto. See X-acto.

Fake. A piece that is misrepresented—i.e., shown or sold as something that it is not. A fake may be constructed as such or it may be a changed piece.

Faking of Woods. This is the general term used to mean finishing a wood to look like wood of another type. This common practice is dishonest only if it is misrepresented.

Fastener, Metal. Any metal device used to hold a joint such as a nail, screw, or corrugated fastener.

Filler. See Wood Filler.

Finish, General. The result of all the things that have been done to and applied to a wood to bring it to its final appearance.

Finish, Specific. The protective coating applied to a surface—e.g., varnish, shellac, lacquer, paint, and oil.

Finish, Type: Clear. A finish that does not obscure the surface beneath —e.g., varnish, shellac, lacquer, and oil.

Hard. A finish that is physically hard and quite protective of the surface beneath—e.g., varnish, shellac, paint.

Opaque. A finish that completely obscures the appearance of the surface to which applied—e.g., paint and refinisher's enamel.

Soft. A finish that is relatively soft and offers little protection to the wood beneath—e.g., sealer wax.

Flat (paint). A flat paint is one that has no gloss when dry.

French Polishing. A technique for applying shellac with a cloth. This very high gloss dries almost immediately and is used primarily in restoring.

Furniture, Antique. The generally accepted meaning of "antique" is that such a piece is 100 years old or more.

Furniture, Old. This classification includes pieces that are not aged enough to be antiques but have acquired a value due to age.

Furniture, Used. This is just plain secondhand furniture.

Glorification. This type of fakery includes adding something (carving, inlay, rockers) to a piece to make it appear more valuable.

Gloss. The "shine" of a finish; varies from high to semi to satin to eggshell.

Grain. The pattern of light and dark fibers in a piece of wood.

Hard Finish. See Finish, Type: Hard.

Hardwood. Wood of a deciduous (leaf-bearing) tree. Maple, walnut, and oak are among the hardwoods.

Holiday. A missed area—not covered by finish, for example.

Injector, Glue. A metal hypodermiclike device for injecting glue into hard-to-reach places.

Inlay. See Veneer.

Joint. The place where two pieces are joined.

Kutzit. A recommended no-wash remover.

Kwik. A recommended no-wash remover.

Lacquer. The most fragile of the hard clear finishes.

Lacquer Thinner. The solvent for lacquer—used for thinning, testing, and restoring.

Linseed Oil. See Oil Finish.

Lye. A strong, quick-acting, dangerous, wood-damaging remover. Not recommended.

Maintenance. The process of preserving and extending the life of a finish.

Marquetry. See Veneer.

Match-Staining. The process of matching the effect of a stain to the result of a previous staining.

Milk Paint. An opaque finish made with milk and colored with clay, blood, or berries. (Today we use less exotic coloring ingredients.)

Mineral Spirits. Another name for paint thinner.

Natural Wood. See Finish, Type: Clear.

Neutralize. To stop the action of a chemical substance by using another chemical.

No-Wash (remover). A commercial remover that does not have to be washed off or neutralized.

Oil Finish. A soft/hard clear finish produced by repeated applications of boiled linseed oil or by one or two applications of "Antique Oil" (Minwax).

Oil Stain. A stain (color) in an oil-base vehicle that soaks into the wood carrying the color pigments.

Old Furniture. See Furniture, Old.

Opaque Finish. See Finish, Type: Opaque.

Overcoat. A coating of one material over another; e.g., shellac with an overcoating of varnish.

Paint. An opaque finishing material consisting of color pigments in a vehicle with oil, water, or latex base.

Paint Thinner. An oil-based material used to thin varnish and paint (oil-based).

Paste Filler. See Wood Filler.

Pathfinder. A unique method of locating sequential refinishing processes. Consists of master chart and chapter charts. Found only in this book.

Patina. An intangible appearance of age due to normal wear (use) and the action of light, humidity, and temperature on a wood and its finish.

Penetrating Stain. See Oil Stain.

Plane. See Sandpaper.

Plastic Wood. A brand name for a wood filler material (definition 1).

Poultice. A cloth or paper pad used to apply continuously a liquid with which it is soaked.

Power Sander. See Sandpaper.

Process. See Refinishing Process.

Refinisher's Enamel. The author's special name for a finish consisting of flat paint overcoated with varnish.

Refinishing Process. An integral operation that produces the desired result of a step in a complete refinishing.

Remover. A substance that dissolves a finish and facilitates its removal from a surface.

Reproduction. A replica of an antique. Not made to deceive.

Restoring. Performing those operations necessary to return an old finish to its original appearance.

Rough, in the. An antique or old piece "in the rough" is one in the condition in which it is found without any restoring or refinishing.

Sandpaper. Chisels, planes, power sanders, saws, scrapers, and sandpaper are construction tools not used in refinishing.

Sandwich. See Clamp Sandwich.

Saw. See Sandpaper.

Scraper. See Sandpaper.

Sealer. A substance that seals the pores of wood, preventing the finish from soaking into it.

Sealer-Stain. A substance that both seals and stains wood in one operation.

Sealer-Wax Finish. A soft, fragile, clear finish produced by applying wax to sealer or sealer-stain.

Shellac. A hard clear finish that builds body quickly. White shellac is used in finishing furniture.

Shellac Stick. The best material for filling holes, cracks, and the like. Available in a variety of colors.

Shim. A thin wedge of material (wood, cardboard, metal) used to fill the space between two parts.

Soda-Ammonia. A home-made remover consisting of washing soda and household ammonia.

Soft Finish. See Finish, Type: Soft.

Softwood. Wood of a coniferous (needle-bearing) tree. Pine, fir, and spruce are softwoods.

Solvent. A substance that dissolves another substance. Denatured alcohol is a solvent for shellac; lacquer thinner is a solvent for lacquer.

Stain. A substance used to change the color of wood. Composed of color pigment in a vehicle (oil, water, or other base).

Stripper. See Remover.

Stripping. The process of removing (stripping) the finish from a piece.

Stripping Tank. Common name for several commercial operations that remove the finish from furniture by dipping it into a "stripping tank" containing a chemical solution.

Stripping Vat. See Stripping Tank.

Tank. See Stripping Tank.

Tip Off. To use the tips of the bristles of a brush to smooth an application of finish.

Turpentine. A substance used to thin oil-based liquids.

Used Furniture. See Furniture, Used.

Unfinished Furniture. Furniture that is sold without having been stained and finished.

Varnish. The hardest of the clear finishes.

Varnish Stain. A substance that stains and varnishes in one operation. Not recommended for brush application.

Vat. See Stripping Tank.

Veneer. A thin covering of wood applied to a more common (usually) wood for the sake of appearance and design.

Wash-Off (remover). A remover that must be washed off with water.

Wax Filler. Wax is used to fill holes, cracks, and the like. Available in a variety of colors, wax is easier to use than shellac sticks and is suitable for most repairs.

Wax Stick. See Wax Filler.

Wood Bleach. See Bleaching, Wood.

Wood Filler. (1) A substance used to fill holes and cracks in a wood surface. Available in powder or paste form. Recommended only under opaque finishes. (2) A substance applied to a wood surface to fill the pores and produce a smooth, even surface.

Workshop. A workshop is wherever you refinish your furniture—basement, garage, storeroom, attic, back yard, or wherever.

X-acto (knife). Brand name of a knife with replaceable razorlike blades.

Index

Contact cement, 65
Cracks and gouges, 69–70, 74, 87–88, 99, 132

Decorative painting, 130
Dents, 73, 87
Dexall's Wood Bleach, 56
Drawers, 64, 79; and furniture age, 154, 155–157, 160; hardware, 74, 157; repair of, 70–71; replacement of, 164–165; and varnishing, 109
Dressing, 116–118, 131, 135; maintenance of, 118–122. *See also* Wax
Drop-leaf table, 74–75
Dry sink. *See* Tin

Elmer's Glue, 64–65
Enamel. *See* Paint and paint finish
End grain, 47, 83–84
Equipment and supplies, 6–7; for bleaching, 53–54; for dressing, 117–120, 122; for gluing, 64–65; for staining, 80; for stripping, 34–41; in surface repair, 88, 90, 93; for varnishing, 106–107; in veneer repair, 66–69. *See* also specific entries, i.e., Flashlight; Gloves; etc.
Etch marks, 122

Face mask, 55
Fake furniture, 162–165
"Faking of woods," 18
Fan, exhaust. *See* Ventilation
Finish; defined, 12, 13–15, 23; and furniture age, 152–154; stripping of, 35–46; types, 23–28; and wax protection, 116–122
Finishing, 13, 23
Fir, 19
Flashlight, 151–152
Flat paint. *See* Paint and paint finish
French polishing, 131–132
Furniture, acquisition of, 139–147; age identification, 152–161; fake, 162–165; inspection tool kit, 151; maintenance of, 116–122; new, 13, 116–117, 134–135; replacement of parts, 8, 72–73, 164–165; styles, 140–141, 163–165; used, 141–142, 147; value of, 13–14, 18, 72, 124, 140, 164–165, 169; and varnish, 107; veneers, 19–21; and woods, 16–19. *See also* An-

tiques; Authenticity of furniture; Refinishing; Restoring; Unfinished furniture

"Glorification," 165
Gloves, 40, 41
Glue, 64–65, 68; injector, 67; removal of 64, 69
Gluing, 60–66, 76; of loose joints, 65, 69, 70; of split boards, 69; time required, 63–64; of veneer, 66–69
Gouges. *See* Cracks and gouges
Grain (wood), identification of, 16–19; and shrinkage, 71, 158–159; staining of, 77–79, 81–82; and steel wool, 44, 129. *See also* End grain; Woods
Gum tree, 19

Hard finish. *See* Clear finish; Paint and paint finish
Hardware, 74, 76, 157–158; cleaning of, 122; stripping of, 46–47
Hardwoods, 18
Heat repair, 66, 68
Heirloom varnish (McCloskey), 107–108
Holes, 87–93, 157–158; in fake pieces, 163
"Holidays," 109
Humidity. *See* Water damage
Hydrogen-peroxide, 119–120

Iceboxes, 47
Industrial Cooperative Training, ICT, 183
Ink spots, 47
Inlay. *See* Veneer

Johnson's Paste Wax, 117
Joints; and furniture age, 155–156; gluing of, 60–66, 69, 70

Knife, putty, 40, 43; scout, 151–152
Kwik Liquid No Wash Remover, 36, 39, 40, 43
Kutzit Paint Remover, 36, 40, 43

Lacquer finish, 24, 26–27, 36, 38, 116–117, 134; advised against, 112; characteristics, 105; and furniture age, 153; identification of, 127, 135; on metals, 122; and moisture, 133; in restoring, 127–129, 133; and wax repair, 92
Lacquer thinner, 127–128, 133